Navigating the Labyrinth

Navigating the Labyrinth

Teacher Empowerment Through Instructional Leadership

Shirley Ann Smith

ROWMAN & LITTLEFIELD
Lanham • Boulder • New York • London

Published by Rowman & Littlefield
An imprint of The Rowman & Littlefield Publishing Group, Inc.
4501 Forbes Boulevard, Suite 200, Lanham, Maryland 20706
www.rowman.com

86-90 Paul Street, London EC2A 4NE, United Kingdom

Copyright © 2022 by Shirley Ann Smith

All rights reserved. No part of this book may be reproduced in any form or by any electronic or mechanical means, including information storage and retrieval systems, without written permission from the publisher, except by a reviewer who may quote passages in a review.

British Library Cataloguing in Publication Information Available

Library of Congress Cataloging-in-Publication Data

Names: Smith, Shirley Ann, 1957– author.
Title: Navigating the labyrinth : teacher empowerment through instructional leadership / Shirley Ann Smith.
Description: Lanham, Maryland : Rowman & Littlefield, 2022. | Includes bibliographical references. | Summary: "By using methods in Navigating the Labyrinth, educators can disregard fads and establish a metacognitive process for how they recognize what beliefs they have about how students learn, how they approach research so that it drives instructional decisions, and how they design and deliver instruction that ensures student learning at the highest level"—Provided by publisher.
Identifiers: LCCN 2021058224 (print) | LCCN 2021058225 (ebook) | ISBN 9781475864977 (cloth) | ISBN 9781475864984 (paperback) | ISBN 9781475864991 (epub)
Subjects: LCSH: Effective teaching. | Instructional systems—Design.
Classification: LCC LB1025.3 .S635 2022 (print) | LCC LB1025.3 (ebook) | DDC 371.102—dc23/eng/20220106
LC record available at https://lccn.loc.gov/2021058224
LC ebook record available at https://lccn.loc.gov/202105822

For Ron

Contents

Preface	ix
Acknowledgments	xi
Introduction	1
1: What Do You Believe?	3
2: Is Teaching an Art or Science?	17
3: Have You Done Your Research?	33
4: How Is Learning Assessed During Teaching?	43
5: How Is Effective Instruction Designed?	59
6: How Is Effective Instruction Delivered?	73
7: Where Does Technology Fit?	85
8: Where Do You Go from Here?	99
Bibliography	103
About the Author	107

Preface

For educators, like myself, that have been working in the field of education for many years, the pendulum in our profession is swinging back and forth all the time. There are many reasons this happens—most of them outside the ability of the classroom teacher to control. Reasons such as change of administrators, an education industry with their ever-changing products, or politicians and policymakers changing laws, programs, and accountability measures.

Teachers take these changes in stride but even the good changes seem to take forever—if at all—to reach into the classroom and change teaching practices for the better. Teachers become jaded and decide to either wait the changes out or sometimes, when the stress level gets too much, leave the profession.

As an educator for 40+ years, I have experienced these pendulum swings as a teacher, an administrator, but most importantly, an observer in classrooms. While thought leaders and futurists in education continually write and speak on the big ideas needed to redesign or transform teaching practices, my experience shows that these grand ideas are usually not accessible to teachers. Those big ideas may be "just the thing" that will work in classrooms, but teachers are caught up in a yearly school cycle that leaves little time or inclination to take on new practices, even when those ideas may bring lasting change that benefits student learning.

I believe that the collective power of every teacher in a school, working towards a common goal of improving foundational practices based on research-based evidence, is how a great teacher can be in most, if not all, classrooms. By working on what a teacher can control himself or herself, this vision can be accomplished. But it needs to start with individual teachers. I wrote this book to describe and distill the process needed to make this major cultural shift happen—a process that is accessible to teachers and can be adopted as continual professional growth.

As I continue to visit schools and classrooms, I see the need for this process to happen at all levels, regardless of where the school is located. Educators are always looking for the magic bullet—the one major change in a program, in a leader, or in a policy that will transform teaching. I believe the magic bullet already exists in every classroom—the teacher. But each teacher needs to take a close look in the mirror and boldly examine their beliefs, their attitudes, and their everyday teaching practices. That will be the constant that enables the teaching profession to weather the pendulum swings and restore and regain the teachers' roles as instructional leaders.

Acknowledgments

This book has been in the works for most of my career. Spanning over forty years, I have had the privilege to work with many dedicated educators to form, shape, and influence my career. I am thankful for all of them. I am most thankful for the all the teachers I have had the privilege of working with as an observer, as a coach, and as a friend. The graciousness they have shown when I appeared in their classrooms stays with me to this day.

Before my career, though, I was taught by my German mother, now deceased, that to be a teacher was to be in a noble profession. She also taught me to always do my best and take pride in my work regardless of whether I was ironing a handkerchief or obtaining a higher education degree. I thank her for instilling the self-discipline and desire to always pursue an education.

I am thankful for the two most influential teachers from my K–12 experience, Ms. Annie Grace Gaddy (now deceased), my fifth-grade teacher, and Dr. Joan Assey, my ninth-grade English teacher. Each of them challenged me in ways that made me pay attention and want to learn.

At a first-year teacher at L. W. Condor Elementary School in Richland School District Two, in Columbia, South Carolina, I learned one of the greatest lessons from a mentor teacher, Ms. Sue Jordan, now deceased. I was struggling with classroom management issues as most often happens in the first year. Sue gave me advice that stayed with me my entire career—the children that are least lovable need it the most. I will always be grateful for that advice. Other colleagues that influenced me in my early years of teaching were Pauline Bauguess (now deceased), my first principal, and Dr. Amy Donnelly, a co-teacher that went on to administration and higher education positions. I am grateful for the opportunity to have learned from them at such an impressionable time in my career.

Dr. Harvey Allen was one of my professors in the School of Education at University of South Carolina-Columbia when I was an undergraduate. He later became the chair of my doctoral committee, and I am forever thankful for his guidance, his kindness, and his grace during that time.

Another influence was Gary Vance, my boss at SERC (Satellite Education Resources Consortium). Gary hired me to rewrite a grant, and then later, to direct that project. He provided not only leadership as I learned new skills needed to be a project director of a multimillion-dollar grant but helped me navigate the world of public television. I thank him for his kindness and the respect he showed in always seeking my thoughts and opinions as part of his leadership duties.

Mr. Danny Shaw, now deceased, was a talented educator with national awards by the time I had the opportunity to work with him as a consultant for DataWorks. Danny was kind, generous, and always supportive as we both travelled throughout the south working in schools to improve instruction. He had a gift for making everyone he met feel important and loved. I was privileged to have been his friend and colleague.

In June 2019, when the pandemic was raging and everyone was staying home, I had the privilege of joining a group of academic women who needed time, space, and guidance to write. Led by Dr. Cassie Premo Steele, I met with this group of smart, talented women four times a week for many, many months. The collective writing experience with these women was transformational. It enabled me to not only write this book but gave me so much more acceptance, advice, and affirmation that this was the right thing to do at this time in my life. I will be forever grateful for this experience and these women.

I also want to thank a cousin and friend, Frank Baker, a renowned author, and educator in his own right, known for his work in media literacy. He has been prompting me to write this book for several years, was persistent in his efforts, and even offered his name as an entrée to the publishing world.

Finally, I owe a huge debt of gratitude to my husband, Ron Hagell. He has always been supportive of my career, long before the book writing process began, and is always by my side with love and encouragement. He provides an excellent example of always being willing to learn new things, no matter a person's age. I thank him with all my heart and all my love.

Introduction

Most teachers enter the teaching profession with good hearts and good intentions. They have a love of children that leads them to teaching and a love of learning that makes them passionate about the profession. Most teachers want to make a difference in children's lives and believe, with the right education and training, they can have a positive effect on their community. Within this context, one could say teachers enter a labyrinth of sorts: a twisty path that leads towards a center. A center that includes improved lives for children, leading to a productive and vibrant society.

Imagine all the obstacles along the path that the teacher must navigate however—politics, policies, parents, administrators, lack of resources, societal failings such as poverty, and other bottlenecks—passages that must be traversed to move forward. But there are also passageways that lead the teacher forward despite constraints, passageways that a teacher chooses because it leads them closer to the center. This metaphor is central to the theme of this book—enabling teachers to be the instructional leaders they must be to reach the desired result in spite of the constraints and bottlenecks.

Schooling does not happen in a vacuum and teachers will always encounter "outside" influences on what happens in the classroom. However, teachers can still achieve educators' promises for children by examining themselves, their practices, and making small, but important changes in the process of teaching and learning.

This book has seven chapters. The first three describe bottlenecks that can impede a teacher on their journey. These bottlenecks include teacher belief systems, whether or not teaching is an art or science, and the role of research in the education profession. Collectively, these bottlenecks not only hinder the teacher on her path, but are a strong, silent force behind why it is difficult to make changes to the education structure. For decades, the cry has been that education needs to be reformed, reimagined, redesigned, or whatever is the current word du jour for changing the way we school children. Thought leaders in education have written books, spoken at conferences, and blogged continuously on school change topics, often citing many of the strategies in this book. However, even with all the good intentions, these strategies get lost in the ether and become inaccessible to teachers.

Over the many years of my profession and having been privileged to observe in hundreds of classrooms, I have found that little has changed in how we school children. It is my belief that the sea change needed begins with each teacher doing the hard work of examination of their practices. Breaking down the change process into its smallest parts so each teacher can work to improve their practice is what is needed to truly make a difference in children's lives.

The last four chapters include passageways that a teacher can follow to move closer to the center. When practiced collectively by grade level, by a school, by a district, these passageways can help educators avoid the pitfalls of education reform and enable teachers to restore and retain their roles as instructional leaders.

Each chapter includes at the end a section called "Practical Matters." This section provides teachers and administrators concrete actions to implement and gives a glimpse of what that particular passageway "looks like" when put into practice.

1

What Do You Believe?

Bob Dylan wrote a song about times a-changing, a universal song that at the time applied to societal changes needed for a more just world. But the sentiment is timeless because change is a constant in our world. To be alive is to experience change. As we grow from children to adults, our bodies change, our place of residence sometimes changes, our choice of career and life pursuits can change, our relationships evolve, and even our religion and political perspectives can change. As we experience life, travel, and meet new people, we learn new ways of doing things, seeing things, and we have opportunities to "try on" new perspectives and compare them with our old ones.

Sometimes we feel the changes are happening too fast, sometimes too slowly. Incremental change as opposed to cataclysmic change is a constant tension in life. While we understand that changes require a progression in evolving steps, we also know that a sudden change can be beneficial in some respects as well. That tension is illustrated most starkly in our chosen profession of education.

Educational systems must be able to address change in a multifaceted arena to truly embrace change. This includes examining some system "traditions," addressing rapidly changing classroom needs, and evaluating the human characteristics of educators. Without an honest evaluation of these cogs in the education system wheel, real change is ephemeral.

There are certain standards in the education system that exist primarily because change happens at such a glacial pace. For example, the school calendar where students attend school September through June and then have summers "off," harks back to the agrarian way of life when children were needed to work in the fields during harvest time. State policy makers everywhere instituted the "180-days of school in an academic year" rule which means children really just attend school for half a year.

Despite changes in technology, the increased mobility of families, and ongoing pressure for school to encompass more and more of being in *loco parentis*, this structure for school has not budged. Of course, educators have played around with the number. Some schools started so called "year-round schooling," but it means children go a few weeks, then are off for a few weeks throughout a calendar year.

However, the school year is still 180 days. But this type of schedule interferes with the traditional schedule with "summers off." "Year-round school" can throw off summer schedules for many families—mainly middle-and higher-income families—for summer plans such as vacation and sleep away camps. Also, childcare and other working family issues can be burdensome when children are not attending school for a week at time throughout the year, so it remains unpopular. The "summers off" school schedule has become so entrenched into society as a whole that it will take a powerful political and societal will to change it. It is a given that this change must begin with more availability of quality and affordable childcare.

The difficulty in changing this traditional structure of schooling can be seen more clearly when society thinks about sentimental rituals—some tied to economic structures—that have evolved at the beginning of school. Think of new back-to-school clothing purchases and new school supplies.

Don't we all remember with fondness the shiny new pencil case and lunchbox? There are now "tax holidays" associated with end of summer, school supply drives, and other consumer-driven activities with the back-to-school theme. And what about all those first day of school pictures so common on social media?

Given the emotional attachment society has developed for these events, it is highly unlikely the traditional structure of 180 days of school from September to June will go away anytime soon.

There have some attempts to ameliorate this structure with the advent of charter schools. However, although some charter schools can waive the 180-day-rule and go as long as 175 instructional days, the majority maintain the 180-day-rule. Unfortunately, the original intent of charter schools to "charter a new way" for public schooling has become a political football and research studies show little difference between student achievement in charter schools and public schools.

In the vacuum of more family-friendly policies, schools have been asked to take on more and more: more content, more childcare responsibilities, more medical care, more social and psychological care. These demands have occurred at the same time educators must meet increasing curriculum accountability measures. Parents, extended family, or the "village" once shared these responsibilities, but schools now feed children their meals, provide nursing care, keep children after school, and even provide laundry facilities.

It has been estimated that children spend about 85% of their time out of school, mainly at home. Yet what happens during that home time affects the children that come into our classrooms to learn because children do not leave their troubles at the classroom door. Teachers can encourage parents to read to their children, provide educational experiences, and encourage a positive attitude about learning, yet this does not always happen unfortunately.

While teachers recognize the influence of home on a child's school success, teachers by and large have no say in what goes on outside the classroom for children. Most likely, teachers would rather that aspect of school be left to social workers and parent support organizations. They have their hands full with constant curricular changes, lack of funds for teaching materials, and the parade of new programs and policies each year.

Some changes, such as school schedules, move along at a slow, incremental pace. Teachers experience changes to the curriculum, resources, procedures, and policies on an annual basis. These changes often occur at the beginning of a new school year and are imposed from the top down. Sometimes these program or policy changes in how and what to teach begin strategically and with good intentions, but during the process of implementation, become mechanical gestures, relegated to a checklist. Think lesson planning, teacher evaluations, and teaching reading.

For example, the process used to plan lessons varies by school or districts. The content of lessons is generally designed according to traditional learning theories, then overlayed with new processes when a new initiative such as Growth Mindset, gets popular. This lesson planning process then moves into the format of the lesson plan, it's digital program if one is used, how often it is "turned in" to the principal, how to make it accessible to visitors to the classroom, etc. Lesson planning quickly devolves into a fill in the blank or cut and paste activity rather than a thoughtful planning guide for student learning.

Another example is the path from writing of curriculum standards to writing lesson plans to writing on an analog whiteboard each day. The intent is there—if a teacher connects the daily lesson to a curriculum standard, and it is visible to students and observers, then teachers will stay on track and up to date with the pacing guide and everyone will be ready for the spring testing.

In reality, these good intentions go awry quickly enough when teachers do not "connect" the curriculum standards with a lesson plan but merely cut and paste the standard into the digital lesson planning software, tape the printed-out plan on the door, and write the standard on the board and it stays there until an undetermined time. The mechanical actions overcome the strategic intent and contribute to laissez faire behaviors that can encompass the academic year.

Change—whether it is in daily behavioral actions by a teacher or large-scale district reform—causes discomfort. Discomfort is a necessary component of change. Like a caterpillar breaking out of the cocoon, it requires breaking out of daily habits that may or may not be healthy. Sometimes this change is mandatory in a school, such as when a new textbook is adopted and teachers must learn a new system along with new strategies. Sometimes the change is voluntary like when a school adopts a new learning theory such as project-based learning. The latter is more an exception than rule.

Oftentimes the communication methods used by districts and schools about a change, whether it be curricular or managerial, lacks a cohesive and consistent approach. Even the best laid plans by administrators result in differing thoughts and ideas running rampant among faculty and staff before the change can be implemented. One can either blame or credit the rise of social media in these instances.

While some channels of communication are formal, the informal channels can often breed rumors, resentment, conflict, and confusion. Sorting out the true from the false becomes a challenge for all—those trying to lead the change and those that must implement the change.

Timelines for change are often unrealistic, driven by the aforementioned sacred cow of the academic year. A false goal of having every child accomplish the same standards of learning produce a pressure cooker pace for change. Test scores must rise by the end of the year is the cry. Administrators often sacrifice quality for speed and are disappointed when the change they advocated did not happen in the short time span allotted.

We know that changing behavior is a difficult task. Oftentimes, administrators embark on a new direction with new resources, new techniques, new programs, and expect that students will show success by year's end. Or even in three to five years' time. These new initiatives come and go with new superintendents, new principals, even new school board members. When the desired changes do not happen, where do educators turn? Since teachers are the main conduit of education reform in the education system, they can easily become scapegoats.

The lack of readiness for the change is grossly undervalued by change leaders. This is seen over and over at all levels of education when a new initiative is launched. The system defines change in the form of test scores, teacher competencies, and overall improvement of student learning, but fails to acknowledge that a teacher's behavior must change to allow for needed innovation to take root.

A change initiative that does not take into account what motivates change among both teachers and students, the influences of informal communication channels, and/or cultural entrenchments will doom a change initiative before it gets started. Without an overt acknowledgment of what these influences are, the change initiative will be undermined and treated frivolously by all involved. This wastes time, effort, and dollars. A simple investment into acknowledging and deterring these influences before a change initiative takes place should be a necessary and mandated part of any change initiative strategy.

A needs assessment—an in-depth look at the system—is sometimes taken before a new initiative takes place. However, it is not the same as assessing readiness. A needs assessment is a process usually used to determine priorities, make organizational improvements, and allocate resources. Assessing readiness looks at the influences on that system that can highlight when and where the system has *hidden resistance* to a change. It can be argued that education systems need both types of assessments to realize lasting change.

Schools are occupied by human beings who enter the doors with past experiences, present circumstances, and differing worldviews based on these aspects. Teachers, students, administrators, parents, vendors, all other visitors to a school enter with belief systems. These systems of belief are both subconscious and conscious.

Our experiences shape us, and our belief systems help maintain structure for us. All decisions made during the day come from those structures inside us. The mind-body connection and the complexity of human life is always at work. There are cognitive and implicit biases that filter our decision making. These biases are outside our conscious awareness and are pervasive. They challenge even the most well-intentioned educator and oftentimes conflict with explicit intentions.

There is a trifecta of psychology traits that our brains use to make sense of the world: confirmation bias, cognitive dissonance, and motivated reasoning. These three, when mixed, create a potent recipe for either ignorance or enlightenment. As rational and objective as we humans think we are, we can deceive ourselves in the process of reasoning. This process is subject to influence, or bias, by emotions and instincts.

The first trait is *confirmation bias*—the tendency for people to believe evidence that confirms their preexisting beliefs and ignore information that counters those beliefs. While we naturally want to corroborate our beliefs, it can be uncomfortable and counterintuitive to look for evidence that contradicts them. A classic study in 1979 was carried out by Stanford University researchers to explore the psychological dynamics of confirmation bias. The study was composed of undergraduate students who held opposing viewpoints on capital punishment and were asked to evaluate two fictitious studies on the topic. One of the false studies provided data in support of the argument that capital punishment deters crime. The other supported the opposite view, that it had no effect on overall criminality in the population. Both were designed to give "equally compelling" objective statistics. The researchers found that the responses to the studies were broken down by participants preexisting opinions: participants that initially supported the deterrence argument considered the anti-deterrence data unconvincing and thought the data in support of their position was credible. Participants that held the opposing view at the beginning reported the same, but in support of their stance against capital punishment. What is more amazing is that when confronted with evidence that both refuted it and supported it, both groups were even *more* committed to their original stance, becoming more entrenched in their existing beliefs. The researchers concluded that, "people of opposing views can find support for those views in the same body of evidence."

The second trait, *cognitive dissonance*, is the discomfort of holding two conflicting beliefs at one time. Leon Festinger introduced this term in 1957 after he infiltrated a UFO cult convinced the world would end at midnight on December 21, 1954. These cult members had given up their homes and jobs to work for this cult. When the end of the world did not occur, members were told that their leader had received a message that the God of the Earth had decided that the planet would be spared. The cult members were relieved and continued to spread doomsday ideology.

Although this is an extreme example, all of us do this regularly. For example, one may believe pizza is an unhealthy food, yet still eat it and rationalize the behavior by telling ourselves "It was worth it" or we will "run it off tomorrow." Another example involves smokers: they know it is a habit that can lead to death but continue to inhale. If they have tried to quit and were unsuccessful, they justify the failure as a behavior that is "not that bad" or "worth the risk." All of us hold beliefs that are not consistent with reality but tend to always go with what is most comfortable rather than what is true.

Most of the decisions we make whether conscious or unconscious, are influenced by motivation. We usually have an intended purpose underlying those decisions. But oftentimes those goals conflict with each other. How we balance and prioritize competing goals can determine the reasoning we use, which can result in *motivated reasoning,* or accepting evidence that supports what is already believed. It is used to avoid or lessen cognitive dissonance, especially on topics that relate to comfort, happiness, or mental health. It's easier to dismiss a contradiction that re-examine it. Using the example of smoking again, smokers engage in motivated reasoning when they dispel scientific evidence that smoking is an unhealthy habit. There really is very little difference between these three traits, but they all serve the same purpose. They help to frame the world for each of us so that it makes sense. How we process information and make decisions can become warped through motivated reasoning, when biased reasoning leads to a particular conclusion or decision. Becoming more aware of cognitive functions and their influence on the instructional decision-making in the classrooms is important to teachers' roles as instructional leaders.

Teachers often think they are behaving one way but actually are not exhibiting the behavior they think. This impacts decision making on many levels for the classroom teacher. For example, one of the protocols used to collect instructional process data in a classroom is keeping tallies on who gets called on to answer questions. In a one-on-one with the teacher after the lesson, teachers will say that they called on students randomly and "mixed" it up. When shown objective data, however, the tally that often shows they called on the same students the majority of the time and likely used the questioning strategies as classroom management decisions rather than an instructional decision. (More about this in chapter 4.)

Some protocols include taking a video of a teacher while teaching and then analyzing it together after the lesson. Teachers are sometimes surprised, even flabbergasted, at their decision making. In fact, the impact of unconscious in bias teaching is well documented. All teachers would likely deny any gender stereotyping in their teaching patterns. But this stereotyping exists and persists. One study by Victor Lang and Edith Sand found that gender stereotypes are negatively affecting girls' math grades and positively affecting boys. Girls often score higher than boys on name-blind math tests, but when presented with recognizable boys and girls names on the same tests, teachers award higher scores to boys.

Another example is from the decades-long research of Myra and David Sadker and Karen R. Zittleman. Through thousands of hours of classroom observations, the Sadkers and Zittleman identified specific ways in which implicit and stereotypical ideas about gender govern classroom dynamics. They found, as others have, that teachers spend up to two thirds of their time talking to male students and they also are more likely to interrupt girls but allow boys to talk over girls.

Teachers also tend to acknowledge girls but praise and encourage boys. They spend more time prompting boys to seek deeper answers while rewarding girls for being quiet. Boys are also more frequently called to the front of the class for demonstrations. When teachers ask questions, they direct their gaze towards boys more often, especially when the questions are open-ended.

What a teacher believes about how children learn also impacts his or her instructional decisions. These belief systems are a complicated mix of ingredients that include how a teacher was taught and resorting to those methods when overwhelmed; racial bias that imply that children from certain backgrounds have stereotypical behavior; or experiences with cherry-picked strategies that are used over and over with and without success. Sometimes it's a case of "this is how it's always been done in my classroom," a disregard for "new" ways of doing things, a disrespect for new ideas and/or dislike of the person suggesting them, or even a religious interpretation or politicization of a new policy change that finds its way to the classroom level.

Most change causes discomfort and we try to avoid discomfort whenever possible. Long-held beliefs, bias, and stereotypes that are not acknowledged can be obstacles to change. These beliefs underlie teacher's implementation strategies and cannot be ignored. The first major discomfort may come when educators take a deep dive into their own minds, asking themselves why they make decisions the way they do, what impact those decisions have on their instructional decision making and the overall view of their professional world.

How do we work with all personalities, biases, and other human characteristics when trying to strengthen instructional decision making in the classroom? Establishing and nurturing a culture that acknowledges these attributes exist and impact teacher and administrator behaviors is a first step. Teachers, any of us really, are defensive when someone tells us what we are doing is "wrong." Hence bristling by educators when noneducators think they know how to "fix" education.

It is a herculean effort to be nonjudgmental but a necessary skill that instructional coaches and administrators must learn. The consultant, vendor, district administrator, parent, or others may believe the change is positive but you cannot make someone change his or her mind. Teachers often need to see success, however that is defined, in their own classrooms to do that.

So often educators hear that change must be systemic, meaning across all the systems that manage and support education. This is a huge task and all eyes usually land on policy making as a key ingredient to systemic change. But policy decisions are made by humans with all the aforementioned beliefs and biases present. Unfortunately, teachers have very little input into those changes although they are the ones that must implement and translate those policies into classroom practice. And that translation is a twisted and gnarly path that travels through many people. There are many, many books for educators on navigating that path. Yet most leave out the readiness factor needed before implementation.

Cultivating honor and legitimacy to metacognition, thinking about the thinking, can be a major step in establishing readiness for implementing change. This is true as to whatever level of change is needed, but particularly at the classroom level, where the most powerful changes can be made. Teachers often feel they have no control over policy changes, particularly and feel more and more powerless in the face of policy changes in the past few decades.

However, they can reclaim their power by becoming more metacognitive about their craft and practice. We ask students to be metacognitive about their own thinking using mind maps, study skills, and other techniques. How often do teachers ask it of themselves?

Metacognition is thinking about why we do what we do. In recent years, as adult learning theories have begun to inform professional development, the term reflection has come to be part of asking teachers to think about their craft; in other words, be metacognitive. Oftentimes reflection is asking teachers to think about a recent experience of a workshop or other professional development activity. These reflections assist in helping teachers in relating to new learning experiences. These tasks of reflection also help teachers change their own behavior.

What if we asked teachers to do this as a natural process in classrooms instead of just when a vendor passes out a survey or an instructional coach asks in a monthly meeting? What if instead of assuming things are happening in our classrooms, teachers were always curious about what is at work in our children's brains along with all the influences that bear on how we design and deliver instructional strategies? How do we go from using strategy that has become a bad habit to changing that behavior so that it is more effective to learning? When teachers are being metacognitive as a regular practice, they are planning, monitoring progress, and flexibly adjusting their activities appropriately.

Skills to accomplish this can be taught. But just as teaching new content requires teaching the concept before the skill, metacognitive skills must be understood at the conceptual level and skills practiced on a daily basis. This is true for all new habits that are formed and change is created. This process cannot occur overnight. However, if you start small the change becomes doable. Think about the athlete or musician learning a new skill. It takes daily practice, practice, and more practice to be proficient. This "small changes first" start to implement change is left out too many times.

Changes in instructional design and delivery should go beyond the curricular change. Teachers may learn new skills from a new text, or use a new computer program, but the concepts of designing and delivering effective instruction to improve student learning apply to any new program, regardless of grade level or content.

Teachers must ask themselves what can I control? Teachers may not have much control over school, district, state, or even national policy-making decisions affecting their profession, but they do have almost complete control over how they make instructional decisions and deliver those strategies in the classroom. Imagine a circular labyrinth that includes societal, personal, professional changes, both wanted and unwanted, along the path. Always, the student and teacher will be in the middle, the beginning, and the end.

After the hard work of sorting through the psychological readiness for change and the programmatic or other innovative change is being implemented, administrators must determine what is needed to keep the change strategic, lest it fall into the mechanics of the process and gets lost.

In addition to the lesson plan mechanics mentioned previously, one example is the "bell work" strategy. The intent is to have students enter a classroom, and immediately begin to work so as not to waste instructional time: working from "bell to bell." However, bell work often becomes a classroom management strategy rather than an instructional strategy.

That is not always a bad thing. Children need to start the class period with calm focus and "bell work" assists in getting them "ready to learn." The academic intent of such work may include activating prior knowledge or practicing previously learned skills. By applying metacognition to this activity, teachers can parse out their intentions, acknowledging both the management aspect and the specific academic intent of how "bell work" connects to the lesson that will be presented that day.

PRACTICAL MATTERS

What does it look like when teachers and administrators are figuring out what they believe?

1. Change is always personal. When confronted with having to make a change that may or may not be our choice, the first inclination is to wonder what does that change have to do with me? Even with the best intentions, changes are difficult on both personal and professional levels. So where does one begin?

Teachers must be willing to examine their own behavior to determine their own belief system and how that system impacts decisions made in their classroom. This is perhaps the hardest part of creating an academic school culture that invites new and different ways of thinking about the profession of teaching and how students learn. Some questions a teacher can ask himself or herself include:

- How aware am I of my own biases that may affect my teaching?
- How open am I to trying new ways of doing things?
- Do I regularly ask myself if there another way to accomplish the current academic goal?
- Do I regularly ask myself if there is a way to do things better?
- Do I regularly ask myself why am I doing it this way?
- Do I have any beliefs that affect my worldview negatively that I bring into the classroom?

An educator must be open to understanding his or her own confirmation bias and motivational reasoning. Understanding personal bias will not eliminate it but it could create an environment in which it is clear that understanding bias and its effects is critically important. Do you hold negative stereotypes that impact how you view your students, your colleagues, your administrators, your students' parents? Online tests exist, such as Project Implicit from Harvard University, that can provide you an outside perspective. If you have colleagues you trust, ask them to look for examples of any bias they may be aware of in your behavior.

There are many types of identified cognitive biases. In fact, there are over 100. However, there is a lot of information about the most common ones such as self-serving bias, anchoring bias, blind-spot bias, placebo effect, selective perception, status quo bias, and zero-risk bias. In order to address blind bias blind spots, teachers need to be aware of these biases to prevent them from influencing how they think.

Perhaps a grade level, department, or individuals can identify a few, define them, and provide examples for the rest of the faculty. The best way to prevent cognitive biases from influencing the way you think is by being aware they exist in the first place. Then, by continuously challenging our own beliefs, we can begin the debiasing process—especially when receiving new information.

2. Teachers often have to attend a professional development session for a program/topic that they may or may not be enthused about. They do not feel like they were part of the decision to implement this new program, textbook, or the latest fad du jour and resent their time being taken for something they did not want in the first place. Maybe they are even thinking how they can get their papers graded or how to check their email during the presentation. Keep in mind that the presenter is only there to represent the program or innovation, not to pass judgment on teachers. Please do not kill the messenger. Be kind, inquisitive, attentive, and polite.

Teachers can do some research prior to the session if possible and think about how the new innovation may or may not meet the needs of their students. They can prepare questions to get to answers that will help with making meaning of the change for them and their students. Above all, teachers keep a willing spirit and an open mind. There may be some nuggets of knowledge, truth, or insights that could help in the adaptation of a teacher's current situation.

Teachers can also be prepared to challenge their own assumptions about the product, innovation, or policy. Assumptions are thoughts taken for granted and believed to be true. They are not facts; they are based on past experiences. If teachers are feeling resistant towards the new thing, whatever it is, it is probably because they have had a bad experience such as a presenter was unkind, or they tried new products that turned out to not be a good fit for their students or they perceived the new product or innovation as a waste of time.

They may have lost enthusiasm and now become emotionally disengaged when yet another new shiny thing is introduced. Acknowledging and challenging assumptions can help teachers take different steps that can yield different results. "Your assumptions are your windows on the world," said Isaac Asimov. "Scrub them off every once and a while, or the light won't come in."

When thinking about all the tasks required of teachers, one often imagines a pile of plates stacked precariously, one on top the other. The thought of one more task, one more new process or strategy to learn, will send the pile crashing down. But what if teachers turn that mindset around and look at the situation as adding to a place setting for the dinner table instead?

Teachers can ask how this change may integrate with what is already working well in their classroom. They can ask during a presentation what information is needed to understand how it works and how it will look in their classroom when implemented successfully. Determine how it will work with the demographics of your classroom, and the other aspects of instruction in a teacher's control, keeping an open mind so these classroom specifics do not become excuses but rather explanations for why or why not it is a good fit for their classroom.

At this point teachers are probably thinking, "Well, it's nice for you to say, you do not have tons of programs being thrown at you all the time with no additional planning time to absorb the new ways." Remember what teachers control. They control their attitude and the metacognitive process adopted to improve your practice. And they control what practices they can let go of to make room for a better one. Teachers often hang onto old strategies like they hang onto old resources, but both need constant examination as to their effectiveness and viability for student learning.

3. Administrators can play a key role in helping teachers change their thinking. They can develop skills that support and help teachers but this role requires a willingness to observe, reflect, and consider new possibilities. They must start with themselves and examine the bad habits of their own practices. Name them, own them, and work to change them. Principals, instructional coaches, and others responsible for supporting teachers must make a nonjudgmental assessment of their habits and provide time, space, and other resources to teachers as they make changes.

Change does not happen in a vacuum. Context and culture are important to implementation of a new innovation. Rather than trying to implement change in a large way, break the change components down into smaller parts so everyone can work on it. Some teachers may need to work with small changes that lead to a larger change while some may grasp concepts of change sooner and can mentor others.

Understanding these dynamics and making them work in favor of success is something leaders can do with delegation and trust. For example, instead of having an observation form with 20 different items to see when you walk into a classroom, choose only a few on the feedback form. Make these a school-wide goal. Ask teachers how they might want to refine those goals to meet their own personal growth goals or their own metacognitive process.

Be aware of where your school, individual teachers, and parents are on the readiness scale and support and differentiate for those teachers that need it. For an in-depth look, use a tool such as the Readiness Thinking Tool (RTT) created by the Wandersman Group (wandersmancenter.org/defining-readiness) to help identify barriers and facilitators of change for your school.

Administrators can also join with a researcher to create focus groups to question change readiness. Focus groups provide a qualitative context and enable school leadership to extend a wide reach to stakeholders beyond teachers such as students or parents. Since confidentiality is an important consideration for working with focus groups, an outside, independent facilitator is needed. Independent facilitators can allow for candor in the focus groups and ensure trust is a key factor.

Focus groups questions can center around history, need for change, willingness to change, faith in leadership, change plan, and skills necessary to implement said plan. In his book *Leading Change in Your School,* Douglas Reeves provides a change readiness continuum rubric using those domains. Although convening these groups and analyzing their responses requires a thorough process, administrators can set this process in motion to inform his or her support for change in their school. Communication with teachers about results will also strengthen the culture of change.

Creating positive culture change on the administrator's part is about differentiating based on each teacher's place on that readiness continuum and mindset for change. But you must start with yourself and share this with your faculty to build trust and ownership.

4. *The education world is filled with jargon, acronyms, and maxims.* Each person in a school internalizes these differently based on their own experiences and filters. Maxims such as "All children can learn" show up in district mission statements and school wall murals. It is important to be sure everyone in a school is working on the same meaning of those jargon words or maxims.

Remember those vocabulary squares elementary teachers use so children can learn new words? They usually have a sheet of paper divided into four parts. Each part has a purpose. For example, usually children are asked to write the word and its pronunciation in the first square, define the word in another square, use it in a sentence in one, and draw a picture in another.

To get everyone on the same page, teachers and administrators ask everyone to do a vocabulary square with words such as "evidence," "success," "systemic," "metacognition," "critical thinking," and so on, as a faculty activity.

Words in a school's mission statement or use some current jargon such as "personalized learning," "differentiation," or "data driven" can also be used. There are several ways each of those terms could look in a classroom. But putting them all on the table makes the matter of expectations and accountability take on new perspectives.

Faculties can do this exercise not so much to learn new words but rather to see how everyone differs in their own interpretations of a word. Usually, those words are ones said every day in education as part of its own academic language and assumptions are made that everyone agrees on their meanings. This activity seems elementary, but once started, everyone will be surprised how those assumptions will be challenged which can lead to meaningful professional conversation.

For example, this exercise was conducted with a district office leadership team at the beginning of a three-year plan to implement a 1:1 program. The participants listed words or phrases that were written in a mission statement about technology. A common term in these types of statements was "students will be engaged." After completing vocabulary squares individually and then discussing their work in small groups, it turned out that many educators had completely different ideas about what that phrase meant to them and what it looked like when it was happening in a classroom.

Until they acknowledged this and had a discussion, they were all going on their own assumptions that everyone else was thinking the same way they do.

This is a simple exercise that yields powerful results. It gives context to have conversations about differences among staff, administrators, and almost certainly parents. Until these differences are brought out into the open, acknowledged, and owned, they will impede change for individuals and schools.

5. Administrators are responsible for maintaining positive morale when change is being implemented. It doesn't take long for "initiative" fatigue to set in and teachers' morale lags. Teachers also become jaded when they perceive that the new innovation will fade away in time. Administrators must pay attention and put into place activities, coaching sessions, conversations, and other leadership methods to maintain a positive attitude. This can only be accomplished if principals are regularly in classrooms, talking to teachers and students on a regular basis, and attending coaching sessions.

Administrators must present themselves as nonjudgmental and willing to help. It is paramount that they have had some instructional practice experience and be able to relate to teachers' issues around instruction.

2

Is Teaching an Art or Science?

Ahhh . . . summer. Most children look forward to the beginning of the season, mainly due to the entrenched culture of "summers off" that was discussed inchapter 1 and all that it entails. Although we know it is not true for many children, the myth of "summers off" brings long, languid days to play, explore, go on a vacation, and to not worry about schoolwork. For teachers, the end of the school year is a chance to relax from a school year full of lesson plans, testing, and meeting daily demands of children and administrators.

However, "summer" is often a short-lived relaxation time because most teachers then dive straight into taking graduate classes, embarking on second jobs as camp counselors or such, working on district committees, and other job-related activities. In fact, most teachers often have to continually dispel the crazy notion that teachers are not teachers between June and August!

August soon rolls around and teachers feel refreshed, ready to begin a new year with renewed enthusiasm and energy. As an elementary teacher, it means time to make preparations for the new school year, whether it be a newly assigned classroom or the same one packed with boxes from the previous year. Floors in schools are shiny from the custodial staffs' efforts during the summer, desks are piled in a corner waiting to be arranged according to the latest ideas from Pinterest, and class lists are disbursed from administration with students you may know but mostly ones you looked forward to meeting.

Elementary teachers especially work to create doors and walls with students' names and what they hope are welcoming themes with bright colors. Posters go up on walls, along with ABC charts, word walls, and various other items that teachers use to decorate their classes. Reading areas are set up with rugs and bean bag chairs. Centers are established for writing, science, technology, and other curriculum areas where students will work independently. After the school year begins officially, anchor charts go up on walls, rules and consequences for behavior are established, and classroom "job" charts are displayed.

In middle and high schools, the old standby notion that the focus is more on content than children come into play. There are fewer decorated bulletin boards and learning centers are replaced with rows of desks. Some attempts are made to establish independent reading areas but mostly these are only bookcases with books that students take back to their desks to read. Students are larger at this age and there are less choices about how to arrange the desks for multiple settings.

Teachers usually have little to no storage space in their classrooms. Teachers take advantage of the vertical space, piling boxes on top of boxes with materials most keep for years and, in some cases, decades. Given that teachers often do not know what grade they are teaching at the elementary level or the availability of new resources, they tend to hoard resources. There are also procedures and processes to teach students at the beginning of the year—how to stand in line, walk down the hall, and turn in homework.

It is easy to get caught up in the rule following conformity that both teachers and administrators feel they need for order. Commercial programs for behavior management, reward systems, and developing consequences have taken root in schools and result in clothespins on name charts to designate times a student has broken a rule, color charts like stop lights, and lists of what will happen when rules are broken.

It is in the beginning of a new school year that veteran teachers tell brand new teachers to establish classroom management skills now and set the tone of respect. Easy to say and hard to do for new teachers. In fact, discipline is the number one reason teachers give for leaving the profession.

As the school year progresses, time is marked by the holiday and testing schedule. With all the additions to what schools are responsible for teaching, the number of days children are in school have not changed—still only 180 days in most places. Teachers have pacing charts, benchmarks, and other tools to keep them on track lest summer rolls around again without completing the curriculum standards for that grade. The load grows every year.

Although curriculum is revised periodically, one constant change is that something will be added. Often additions to the curriculum standards are added via legislatures and State Departments of Education. These include content such as ethnic studies, racial justice, Holocaust studies, sex education, media literacy, coding, and civics education. In addition, there is an overlay of teaching 21st-century skills, emotional intelligence skills, and other "soft" skills such as conflict resolution and work ethic.

No one will argue that these are not worthwhile topics for study in the classroom but many of them are already inherent, if not directly built in to the current curriculum. What does not happen is *removing* any content standards in the curriculum. Yet no time is added to the school calendar or alternative ideas provided for restructuring schooling to accommodate these new areas of study. After many decades of this phenomenon, it's no wonder teachers always operate at high speed to accomplish the contents of their pacing charts.

Regardless of where a school is located, it is possible to observe the arc of the year no matter the grade, location, or subject. Whether walking through the halls, sitting in classrooms, or talking to faculty, it is noticeable when teachers are on auto pilot. This usually happens once the excitement of the beginning of school wanes and lasts until Thanksgiving. Then time is spent "catching up," crunching data, and prepping for the midyear testing cycle that begins in January, when time seems to be going by even faster. It often brings to mind the old adage about the "hurrieder" one goes the "behinder" one gets.

The crunch time really comes around March and April when teachers need to know who has mastered standards, who needs a little help, and who needs a lot of help to complete the year. With draconian accountability measures in place to determine who gets to be promoted, there is a lot of pressure on teachers and students to perform well. Teachers as well as students that started the year excited and ready to teach and learn, are now exhausted, frazzled, and looking forward to summer.

In addition to what is happening in classrooms when students are there, teachers also have to participate in a myriad of duties, meetings, and other activities when students are not in the classroom. And in the midst of all the administrative and housekeeping duties, teachers squeeze in professional development in all forms. Consultants on-site after school, conferences, graduate courses, Saturday workshops, and more.

When teachers are learning to be teachers, much emphasis is put on foundations of education, learning theories, and how to teach reading if you are an elementary teacher or content if you are a middle or high school educator. Once neophytes are put into a classroom, all this usually goes out the window. Days are filled observing mentor teachers, lunch duty, and learning the "lay of the land." Most of their energy is put into classroom management.

Survival becomes paramount and these new teachers realize the fun lesson plans developed in the abstract for a university class assignment becomes something different when real students are sitting in front of them. When "thrown to the wolves," teachers have to rely mainly on instinct. Relying on previous teaching experiences—mostly as a student themselves—influence the unconscious choices made for making instructional decisions. Patterns are set and hard to change once in place.

Is it any wonder that once teachers get in autopilot or survival mode, the teaching profession becomes busywork and less and educators become less mindful about what it means to be a teacher? How do we turn around this arc of the year predictability? The answer lies in the individual teacher knowing what he or she can control, what he or she cannot, and balancing the difference to become a stronger, wiser instructional leader in the education profession. A teacher can begin to do this by analyzing what he knows about his own teaching style and what it is based on.

It is often debated whether teaching is an art or a science or some combination of both. If you search the internet for "teaching as an art and science," you will discover many links and sources. These sources delve into the myriad aspects of teaching and usually label them as one or the other: art or science. The label "science" is used mostly when discussing research on effective teaching, and "art" is used for those characteristics of teaching such as student connection or making the classroom a comfortable environment for students.

Some articles even go as far as saying teaching is not a science at all and lean heavily into the art side. Others try to show a blending of the two in multiple configurations. The two labels, when applied to teaching, falls into the giant pool of education jargon, so the meaning depends on the individual and how he or she filters his or her personal and professional experiences as well as his or her beliefs about teaching.

It can be argued that teaching is some combination of both art and science and is fluid depending on where in the year a teacher finds himself or herself within the arc and mechanisms he or she has put into place to "survive" the academic year. A teacher's personality, philosophy, and approach to teaching, professional experience, and personal flair all go into the art of teaching. Ever since television and *Sesame Street* came into existence, many teachers have felt pressured to entertain children and keep the learning pace going no matter the content so that children are having "fun."

With all of the entertainment and media children have grown up with in these times, teachers are hard pressed to make all content in all grades entertaining and engaging. Technology has sometimes helped this endeavor, but oftentimes hinders the goal. Teachers approach this task of moving content along in many ways, depending on the art of the profession and exude their artistic traits every day with results ranging from effectiveness to chaos.

Into this already stewing mix is added the science of teaching. Teachers have been inundated with a plethora of learning theories developed over decades. Learning theories are an organized set of principles explaining how individuals acquire, retain, and recall knowledge. By studying and knowing the different learning theories, we can know better how learning occurs. The principles of the theories can be used as guidelines to help select instructional tools, techniques, and strategies that promote learning.

Some have been around for decades such as mastery learning or Montessori, with others formed more recently, such as multiple intelligences or project-based leaning. These theories fall into three categories—behaviorism, cognitivism, and constructivism. Although teachers may have learned about these theories in undergraduate courses, think about how many they use currently, have heard of, may use now in some sort of combination, or separately. Think about if or why teachers may use it, how much teachers know about its origins, and whether or not teachers could say *why* they use it.

Behaviorism is repeated actions, verbal reinforcements, incentives, and establishing rules for behavior management, mostly associated with B. F. Skinner. This learning theory is based on the concept of operant conditioning. Behaviorism theorists believe that knowledge exists independently and outside of people. They view the learner as a blank slate who must be provided the experience and observed for changes in behavior to find out what people are learning. Behaviorists believe that learning actually occurs when new behaviors are acquired or changes in behaviors are acquired through associations between stimuli and response. Thus, association leads to a change in behavior.

The behaviorism theory is that learning begins when a cue or stimulus is presented and the learner reacts to the stimulus with some type of response. Consequences that reinforce the desired behavior are arranged to follow the desired behavior. This new pattern can be repeated as it becomes automatic. Examples and applications of this theory in the classroom are drill/rote work, repetitive practice, bonus and participation points, verbal reinforcement, and establishing rules.

These applications also grew along with advances in technology. Drill and practice software is helpful for specific content, such as multiplication tables or second language vocabulary, that must be learned to a level of automaticity. Games and gamification also make use of operant conditioning principles. Acquiring resources and "leveling up" provide reinforcement, while losing one's sword in a battle or falling off a cliff serve to punish errors.

In the 1960s the cognitivism theory of learning, mostly associated with Jean Piaget, gradually began to replace behaviorism as the predominant view. It is not enough to observe behavior, cognitive learning theorists believe, because the internal thought processes are also part of learning. This perspective was heavily influenced by the development of computer technology and telecommunications, and the use of the computer as a metaphor to understand what is happening in the human brain.

Learning in the *cognitivist theory* is defined as storing and organizing information and concepts in the mind. Examples and applications of this theory in the classroom include linking concepts to real world examples, problem solving, discussion, mnemonics, and classifying or chunking information. In 2001, Richard Mayer developed the Cognitive Theory of Multimedia Learning which says people learn better from words and pictures rather than words alone. This theory has influenced the design of media for learning such as using images instead of words, using examples from students' experiences to personalize learning, or combining video, audio, and text.

The constructivist theory of learning, mostly associated with Jerome Bruner, holds that learning occurs as an individual interacts with the environment and constructs meaning by making sense of his or her experience using our own mental models. It emphasizes meaning-making that may be unique for each learner. Constructivist theorists believe that learning is simply the process of adjusting our mental models to accommodate our new experiences.

Constructivism is used to focus on preparing people to problem solve. To be successful, the learner needs a significant base of knowledge upon which to interpret and create ideas. Outcomes are not always predictable and does not work when results need to be consistent. Examples and applications of constructivist theory are case studies, research projects, project-based learning, simulations, and brainstorming. Technology facilitates a constructivist learning experience through tools such as collaborative shared documents, web searches, and projects such as video creation.

These three labels have guided many learning theorists to devise their own version such as Howard Gardner's theory of multiple intelligences, Gagne's conditions of learning, Erickson's eight stages of psychological development, and Maslow's hierarchy of needs. It has been posited that there are at least 50 different approaches to learning including blended learning, self-directed learning, student-based learning, competency-based education, and many more.

Some of these theories are learned in college under the guise of teacher education, but most have been ingrained in teachers by example from their own schooling experiences. Thus, most teachers teach the way they were taught. Unless and until teachers begin to recognize this phenomenon, the science of teaching is buried.

In the past decade, brain research into teaching and learning has grown exponentially. How much of this research makes it into practice is unknown. There are bits of it here and there but along with all other education research about teaching and learning, gets thrown into professional development programs and activities with just enough abandon to confuse teachers each year. Commercial programs sold to districts, make their way to teachers, who implement them as best they can. But this is a haphazard way of putting science into the teachers' "bag of tricks."

Putting theory into practice has been an ongoing theme in education for decades. But the question becomes whose theory? And how exactly does that transition take place, if it does? And what does it look like when it happens? And what happens when theories are cherry-picked and a hodgepodge is created? How are teachers to sift and filter through the morass to find "what works"?

A favorite adage is that teaching is not rocket science—that it's actually much more complex. Teachers do not teach in a vacuum. Swirling around and outside of classrooms are larger, wider circles of influence such as politics, funding, parents, administrators, curriculum, and accountability measures. In public education especially, people bring their own feelings and experiences of school to bear on their attitudes and behavior. Parents especially exemplify this phenomenon. If a parent was not successful in school, a negative attitude toward learning can be passed on to the child.

Funding issues tend to divide schools into haves and have-nots. Poverty-level students bring many issues into the classroom with them that affect what happens in a classroom. Politicians seem to have all the answers without having set foot in a school. Many stakeholders have solutions they think will "fix" the problem only to realize—or not—no one problem exists unto itself. It is wrapped up in numerous layers of society.

To undo patterns of teaching that are not effective and change teacher behavior within the context of a more complex environment, differentiating between what is the art of teaching and what is science of teaching becomes a metacognitive exercise in growing as a professional. Remember metacognition from chapter 1? Here, too, metacognition is important. Metacognitive, thinking about the thinking, means teachers taking it upon themselves to ask what, when? Where? Why? And seek to find the answers through a systematic process, a science centric process if you will, to improve their own practice.

A teacher's passion, charisma, warmth, and humor influence instructional design and delivery. In other words, the art of teaching oftentimes lies in a teacher's personality. But are effective teachers born or made? It takes more than just a love for children to be an effective teacher, more than an exuberant personality. It also takes knowledge and skills in the areas of child development, how the brain learns, content expertise, and pedagogy.

Current models focus on professional development that begins outside school even with the presence of professional communities within schools or school wide book studies. Teachers will most likely tell you they are provided plenty of professional development opportunities on a regular basis. Some are initiated by teachers themselves, but most are provided by administrators that want to "fix" a problem, have been swayed by clever marketing campaigns, or are following some plan set out by "higher-ups." This is not to disregard thoughtful planning of professional development strategies and topics, but to illustrate how even something as important as professional development can switch to autopilot during the arc of the year as well.

Administrators have an important role to play. They keep the lights on, so to speak, and act as a buffer for all audiences that interact with a school—teachers, students, parents, vendors, and all that have business with education facilities. Administrator days are often characterized as constantly putting out fires. Unless an administrator thoughtfully allocates time and attention to minding the big ideas of schooling, they can get bogged down in the minutia.

What if we changed the perspective of professional development from something done to teachers into something driven by teachers? This theme has resonated in many places but not quite taken hold enough to actually transform how teachers teach and students learn. What if the perspective came from scientific research on how children learn and that research was practiced by every teacher and administrator in a school? What if, before and after new programs are bought, new teaching methods are used and new materials are adopted? What if before any innovation is implemented, teachers prepare by asking the questions and doing their own research?

Teachers are the instructional leaders of schools. They must make instructional decisions based on the best information possible. We hear a lot about best practices from every angle, but how much of those come from within the classrooms themselves?

Programs, methodologies, and best practice guides come and go. Sometimes an education "guru" comes along and pulls some practices together from disparate places and creates "new" resources for classrooms. Seems we are always looking for a silver bullet—the one thing that will dramatically change how we teach and learn. The result of this search for the Holy Grail usually results in a hodgepodge of strategies and techniques.

Teachers then bring all the stress of their jobs—and their hopes that maybe this time it is the silver bullet—and sit in the professional development sessions. Yes they still sit, even with what we know about adult learning. Teachers' attitudes range from excited to learn something new to wishing they were somewhere else to downright rude on occasion. They usually feel no control over the topic, the presenter, or choice in using whatever is being put forth. While there are exceptions to the rule and there are some education organizations trying to change the culture, most professional development proceeds along this path.

Teachers make hundreds of instructional decisions in the course of the day. In fact, many of these decisions are made at high speed—literally in the moment. Some are directly related to a particular lesson plan such as stating a learning objective or what specific resource will be used to teach a concept or skill. But many decisions are on "on the fly," in the moment of interaction with a student. A teacher using metacognitive skills will use a combination of skills to address an interaction, sometimes almost unconsciously. This ability requires pedagogical skills that are intentional and meaningful.

A metacognitive teacher will know the difference between a classroom management decision and an instructional decision, and where they may overlap. This knowledge of the science of teaching is the professionalism of our craft.

Teachers also need to be sensitive to the child and the learning environment. Teachers make instructional decisions using three data points he or she usually knows well. First, a teacher uses what he knows about a particular student, his or her personality, his or her learning challenges, or perhaps his or her personal story. Second, a teacher evaluates what the academic data story reveals about that child such as his or her reading Lexile level, test scores, potential learning disabilities, or other learning challenges.

Finally, the teacher knows the relevant learning environment, such as what else is happening in the classroom, home, or remote location outside the classroom which may influence the interaction between teacher and student. This is heavy brain work for a teacher and a hidden cause of why teachers are so tired at the end of the day.

This combination of factors that go into instructional decision making is why there are not always pat answers to what is going on during a lesson. Yet these critical interactions between teacher and student are a necessary element in the developmental process of teaching and learning. A student can learn on his or her own but a teacher needs a learner.

While the art of teaching is the human element, the science of teaching is the teacher putting in the work to improve his or her practice. However, when teachers are subjected to new programs, new resources, new administrators, new rules each year that they teach, it is understandable that they become fatigued—actually jaded—to new ideas to improve their teaching. It is hard to invest time and effort in a new program the new superintendent thinks will "transform" a school, when another one—superintendent and program—will almost inevitably be launched next year.

Teachers cannot control the parade of new administrators or new programs that appear each year but teachers do control the instructional decisions they make on a regular basis. Becoming smarter about how these decisions function in the classroom and their relationship to student learning is an important focus for teachers—and the administrators that lead them.

A systemic approach to enabling teachers to focus more on the science of teaching would require a fundamental change in how schooling is structured. Until some of the "sacred cows" of education are changed wholesale, such as the 180-day-rule, arranging desks in a row in a classroom, inequitable resources, weak teachers teaching the neediest students, homework, grading systems, then it is up to teachers themselves to take on the task of becoming a teacher scientist. Administrators who lead them can support the effort. Leadership is especially important so that changes are systemic rather than piecemeal.

There may be some of you shaking your head about now and want to point out that teachers' days are already filled with new and necessary tasks. Where will teachers find the time and energy to take this on? As with any change, the individual asks, "What's it for me?"

Teachers periodically feel powerless. They feel beaten down by foolish government policies, scapegoated by the public, and oftentimes feel unsupported by parents and administrators. It is easier to keep your head down, lest it get whacked off by the current outrage. Schools do not operate in a vacuum. They are intertwined and integrated with the community and the demographics of their students. This integration inevitably scales out to the broader world of city, state, country, and world.

Yet at the same time, teachers demand higher pay, want to be accepted as professionals on par with others such as engineers and accountants, and generally seek more respect than they are given. The baby step in that direction lies within each teacher, finding the willingness to have an open mind and the courage to assert his or her power as the instructional leader in the classroom.

When teachers take on the mantel of instructional leader and teacher scientist, they begin to ask the right questions, querying the parade of outside consultants, vendors, and even administrators. Teachers can, and do, ask the right questions that come from knowing what works in the classroom and what doesn't, using what they know about the current knowledge base on how students learn and how any innovation informs instructional design and delivery.

Teachers need a curiosity to seek out answers they do not have and the courage to acknowledge that more learning on their part is required. This process should be ongoing, supported, and exalted. Passive-aggressive tactics from teachers will not move this idea forward. Nor do confrontation tactics. An open mind is needed, a curiosity about what the new "thing" has to offer, a curiosity about how it may or may not be applicable to teacher and student learning along with why or why not can lead teachers towards renewing and retaining their role, indeed, owning instructional leadership.

This ownership, before seeking outside information, must first begin with an inward introspection—a curiosity about one's own self and the workings of our own minds and brains. A close look at where instincts come from and how they perpetuate our instructional decision making. *This is perhaps the hardest part of becoming a powerful instructional leader—the self-awareness that is necessary to move forward.* This look in the mirror is hard no matter where you are in life in general, and especially in the teaching profession. Teachers are the experts in their classrooms and like control of what happens there.

But there is so much that cannot be controlled—where students spend their time outside of the classroom, who their parents are, what policymakers and administrators are deciding about teacher's work. However, teachers do have it in their power to control attitudes, behaviors, and efforts in becoming better teachers. When something is amiss in the classroom, it is often easier to blame others—parents, administrators, the "system"—without acknowledging the teacher's role.

Once a teacher has committed to moving in this direction, the next step is revisiting the Education Research 101 course that most, if not all, took "back in the day." For some it was a long time ago. For newer teachers, maybe a couple of years ago. However long ago it was, the research we learned then had no context. As students in preservice, budding teachers had little to no classroom experience, and these research classes were usually in another college—not education—with unfamiliar professors.

Those professors often made little to no connection of the subject matter to the teaching profession, so these courses only presented abstract ideas with no basis in reality. By the time preservice teachers were in their own classrooms, their lives were caught up in the whirlwind of actually teaching. Days were consumed with lunch duty, lesson plans that followed a formulaic pattern, and the drama of real live students became their reality. It's no wonder things like intermittent practice and statistics got buried under benchmark testing and data-driven curriculum.

However, the basis for understanding how students learn, come from those research courses. Questioning strategies, classroom management decisions, ordering of lesson plan elements, creating tests and quizzes, are fundamental activities in education design and delivery. Without understanding the basics of the science of teaching, teachers get caught up in the cherry-picking among professional development practices and relying on past strategies.

Teaching is a social construct. But it is influenced and informed by many types of sciences—psychological, physiological, neurological, biological. This is why it is more complex than it looks like from the outside. Educators are not dealing with widgets, but little people with hearts, minds, and bodies. So much of teaching is wrapped around that idea. Teachers are so connected to these little people that sometimes new ideas for teaching that seem "not to apply to my students" gets discarded by teachers on a regular basis.

The understanding of this psychic connection teachers have with their students is often left out of reform efforts or other innovation initiatives. Sometimes it is referred to as teacher "buy-in," meaning a teacher needs to feel connected to the innovation. However, it is a much deeper notion, one where the teacher needs to make a connection between the innovation and what she thinks is good for her students. Yet, oftentimes, what a teacher thinks is good for his or her students is based on intuition, a much less trustworthy indication of what may or may be good for student learning.

A metacognitive teacher, however, will be aware of where and how her intuition originates and has done the hard work to question if his or her intuition is true or merely based on assumptions. Once a teacher begins to question his or her own assumptions and declares that a change in himself or herself is needed, the even harder work of changing her own behavior begins. As anyone who has tried to lose weight, quit smoking, or otherwise change bad habits knows, this is easier said than done. It requires the enlistment of colleagues that can help define what changes are needed, set goals for the change, and monitor accountability measures.

Readiness to implement a change—whether it be for an individual teacher, a school, a district, or even an entire profession—is an important component to evaluate. Oftentimes, when the directive for change comes from above, and teachers are not vested in that decision, the directive fails. Having a supportive culture for change—one that accepts that failures are indeed learning opportunities—cannot be stressed enough. The ability to cultivate and support change efforts in individuals is a needed trait for all school leadership personnel.

Understanding the change process should be an important overt function of any new program, process, or innovation a school or district undertakes. It should be a meaningful consideration for all decision makers and requires the input—always—of those that will be implementing, namely the teachers. Changing behaviors is not pretty and is hard to do. One needs to have the best information available, open minds willing to take on new ideas even if they are not congruent with current instincts, and a willingness to fail and learn from failures to move forward and be successful.

PRACTICAL MATTERS

What does it look like to examine whether teaching is an art, a science, or both?

1. Be kind. Be kind to yourself first. Do the self-care things necessary to give yourself a clear mind, a healthy body, and a more open mind. These may include regular exercise, eating healthy most of the time, talking things out with your closest friends and colleagues without devolving into gripe sessions, and having fun times regularly with your family and loved ones. Set a goal to be kind to colleagues, including those difficult to get along with, especially administrators.

Share stories about how everyone came to be a teacher and listen to other's stories. This is especially important when the story comes from a burned-out colleague, or from one that has become so bitter and jaded that it is hard to believe he or she was ever a bright-eyed, excited beginning teacher. Ask administrators how they came to be on their career paths, who were their helpers along the way, what have they learned on their path through the maze, what their thoughts and beliefs are about how teachers and students learn.

It will not only help you see colleagues in a different light but will also help clarify thoughts and philosophies of teaching. Maybe this intentional effort will conjure up some memories of being a bright-eyed, excited new teacher which are often forgotten after the weariness of the day-to-day, year-to-year grind.

Be kind to the outsiders who visit the classroom and school: parents, district administrators, consultants, vendor representatives. Assume they have no secret agenda, only a desire, like all teachers, to be a better educator, a better parent, a better friend. This is especially hard given that teachers feel they are always being evaluated, checked on, and judged. This is a consequence of the accountability system that puts teachers in categories with checklists.

What if we changed our perspective and assumed everyone who came into our classroom wanted us to be a better teacher so we could ask them questions and discuss strategies and results without prejudice? A little too Pollyannish? Perhaps. But remember a person can only change himself or herself. An individual cannot make others change. But that individual sure can be an inspiration to others.

This new attitude will take practice and time. It is said that a new habit can be formed in 21 days if practiced daily. Go ahead and say hello and smile at that grumpy teacher down the hall. Every day for 21 days. See what happens.

2. Dig out that old Education Research 101 book from undergraduate school. If it is long gone, go online. There are tons of papers, books, articles, and summaries that go into the basics. Refresh your memory about different types of practice that improve learning, the difference between medical and social research, the meaning of cognitive load and its role in memory processing, how individual and situational interests affect what we pay attention to, what exactly is involved in making memories, how short-term and long-term memory differ, and other processes in the brain that you once knew about but may have forgotten.

Think about how this new-old knowledge applies to decision making about designing instruction and delivering instruction. Not specifically at this point, but generally. Recognizing there is a connection between all these things is a good way to revive curiosity and maybe even get excited again about teaching.

Get reacquainted with how tests and surveys are constructed, how questions are written, different types of tests and why and where they are administered, and how results can be interpreted in different ways for different reasons.

Digesting this new-old information will take time. During the process of revisiting old terms and information, add in new information discovered in the past few years on how the brain works. Not from highly technical resources, but from those that explain new ideas and findings in a way that can be understood.

3. Design a simple action research project for the classroom. This action plan is about a change a teacher wants to make and the action that teacher will take to find a solution to a problem. The research conducted provides a better understanding of the learning environment in your classroom.

Review research literature that speaks to what makes a good research question. Perhaps it's a question about something happening in the classroom that a teacher has noticed and is wondering about. Perhaps a teacher has read an article or heard a consultant say that teachers call on boys more than girls and you are wondering if that occurs in classrooms at your school. Perhaps the research question focuses on a small group of children or an individual child. Identify a problem around issues such as classroom management, curriculum implementation, or instructional strategies that teachers can connect to.

Develop a plan of action. What steps will be taken to find solutions? Is extra reading about it needed? Are colleagues needed to assist in any of the steps? Set out the steps to take with a timeline to stay focused.

Next determine what type of data is needed and how it will be collected. This data can come from student work, or maybe paperwork such as attendance forms, interviews, or maybe questionnaires. The one thing to keep in mind is that meaningful data from various data points can tell a story about an individual but data in and of itself is inert. Data just sits there until a teacher uses his or her professional judgment, his or her knowledge of the student, and his or her knowledge of the relevant literature to make an analysis and interpretation.

As teachers move through this process, they should not be afraid to modify their theories and make adjustments to the collection methods. This will sharpen a teacher's own research and will be invaluable in his or her quest to use more science to be a better teacher.

Administrators can support their faculty in taking these steps in many ways. They can provide the space and time for teachers to review education research, develop action research plans, bring in experts to help navigate the process, and even join in by having an action research plan of their own.

4. *Explore the science of teaching by exploring semantics in your school.* Use vocabulary squares, or another vocabulary tool, and explore how everyone defines various learning theories. A good list of 32 learning theories can be found at www.teachthought.com.

Teachers can also review teaching strategies they use and map them to learning theories which will reveal their own understanding of those theories.

5. *For the purpose of putting more science into teaching, have ongoing conversations about what makes an effective teacher.* This is an age-old question that tries to get answered every time policymakers develop a new instrument to try and measure effectiveness. How often do teachers define for themselves what makes a "good" teacher? Are the words "good" and "effective" synonymous? Administrators may have different ideas about what

a "good" teacher looks like in the classroom that informs their own belief systems for evaluation of teachers—either on paper or in their perception.

In a statewide evaluation instrument many years ago, one of the items to be "checked off" was "sense of humor." It could be argued that this item falls into the art of teaching. Some teachers' personalities lend themselves to humor and others not so much. But someone determined that it fell into the science of teaching because it supposedly makes a teacher more relatable to students and therefore a child would be more willing to learn from her. It was painful to watch teachers try and add this item to instruction when humor was forced. In times such as these when jobs and salaries are attached to these evaluations, these conversations are needed more than ever.

6. *With all the emphasis made on the science of teaching, it is important to remember that teaching is* also *a performing art.* After all, teachers, as well as performing artists—actors, musicians, dancers, trapeze artists—want to engage their audiences. Teachers want to draw students into their orbits, to entertain, to teach, to relate. Elementary teachers know the attention span of their young students is short and they need to have a "bag of tricks" to not only get students' attention, but keep it as long as possible.

Middle and high school teachers are dealing with students that have physical, social, and biological changes coursing through their lives and bodies. These teachers perhaps have a difficult task to get and keep their students' attention.

Teachers want students to love the subjects they are teaching and, more importantly to love learning. Most teachers—although there are exceptions—liked school and did well at school when they were young. It is hard to imagine someone not liking school. But these students are in our classrooms, and we must find a way to relate to them, to move them from apathy to interest. This aspect of teaching often makes teachers uncomfortable, thinking they need to bring a show biz quality to their teaching. But educators must get past that fear and use discomfort to create the energy needed for both teacher and student to do just that.

Talk to the theater teachers, the chorus directors, or the marching band directors. Ask them how they engage students, how they teach students to engage audiences. Maybe a teacher's personality does not lend itself to dressing up in historic costumes if he or she is a history teacher, but thinking about how to relate to students and spark their interest combined with what you know about the science of teaching can be a powerful combination and juncture on the path to becoming a better and more effective teacher.

3

Have You Done Your Research?

Every August there is an excitement about the new school year. "Summers off" is supposed to renew teachers, reinvigorate students, and excite parents, at least, to get children back into a regular routine. The few weeks before children enter the school building, teachers are busily preparing their rooms, gathering supplies and resources, and attending meetings about old and new procedures, policies, and protocols.

In the few weeks before children arrive, there are district level events with motivational speakers and district administrators leading cheers as well as other welcome back gatherings. It's the last chance teachers will have to eat lunch with their colleagues and have time to chat during lunch. Inevitably, there will be professional development sessions to introduce new programs, textbook series, and curriculum guides that were purchased or developed over the summer. Educators accept that this is the way and go through the paces as they await the arrival of fresh faces in the desks they have arranged in their classrooms.

Presenters at these professional development sessions can attest to the enthusiasm and excitement teachers have for a brand-new school year. In looking at the new programs being introduced, it isn't hard to see that many are the same ones that have been introduced over the past several years, although now perhaps with a new logo, a new brand, a new redesign. How are these programs and innovative ideas chosen, by whom, and what input have teachers had in the decision? How long it will take before the bloom is off the rose and teachers settle into old ways and jadedness, boredom, or survival mode sets in?

Education above most other professions has a great tendency to try to reinvent the wheel, to repackage things and present them as new and improved and administrators and teachers just go along. Education research has been around at least 100 years, yet how much of it do we take in as educators and actually use to make our practice more effective? Every now and then "theory into practice" is mentioned but it's not a foundation of how we design and deliver learning for students. Education research can sometimes be found in the materials that are used to market products but is lost by the time the materials reach the classroom level.

Since the 2002 enactment of the No Child Left Behind Act, the terms evidence based, scientifically based, and research based have come into focus. This emphasis on research-based practice in federal law has enabled educators to see research and evidence as a core part of their teaching. If not becoming researchers themselves, teachers are most certainly consumers of research as evidenced by the resources they use in the classroom. With clearinghouses, such as the federally backed *What Works,* that review products, programs, practices, and policies, teachers now have an array of resources to find information to make evidence-based decisions.

As many educators have discovered, however, is the pursuit of this information of what programs and products are evidence based, and the translation of this research in practice, is not straightforward. It can be complex, contradictory, biased, and sometimes just plain wrong. However, a concerted effort must be made by all teachers to not write off this important core of teaching. But to embrace it and figure it out so that learning about and applying effective education research in their practice becomes natural.

Educators often take the most recent education research or a recycled version of past research and rush to apply it in the classroom. Driving the rush are vendors who are quick to monetize the latest education research, oftentimes overpromising when there is not enough evidence of effectiveness and under delivering by not adapting methods backed by scientific research. When put into the context of the arc of the school year and the rush to have improved results in accountability by June, it is clear that educators must take the time needed to learn about which education practices work best and what empirical data indicates about which practices are most effective.

Sometimes new research analysis comes to light can debunk previous research but it's difficult to "put the cat back into the bag." One example of this is the continuing belief about learning styles, the scientific claim that different people have preferred ways of learning. The most frequently referenced styles are visual, auditory, and kinesthetic. Visual assumes that some individuals learn best by looking at pictures, auditory emphasizes others learn best by listening, and kinesthetic assumes still others learn best through hands-on activities. The assumption that students have distinct learning styles and learn best through these channels has influenced teacher practice for decades despite a lack of evidence that such styles even exist.

Like many misconceptions about learning and the brain, the belief in learning styles stems from an incorrect interpretation of valid research findings and scientifically established facts. For example, it is true that different types of information are processed in different parts of the brain. It is also true that individuals have differences in abilities and preferences. Since the 1970s, however, systematic research reviews and meta-analyses examining the validity of differences in learning styles have come to the same conclusion: despite the intuitive appeal, *there is little to no empirical evidence that learning styles are real.* Yet in the education community, the myth persists. This type of dispelled education theory is sometimes called a zombie idea: it keeps returning to life even though its death has already been declared.

Curricular programs in today's schools produce a lot of data. Teachers are expected to take all that data, make sense of it, and use it to make instructional decisions. It is an overwhelming expectation for most teachers. Although the past decade has brought about more data-driven decision making, how many educators have the opportunity to really understand how that data is gathered, how it is interpreted, analyzed, and generalized across school populations? We often make huge leaps in analysis of data, which can lead to making assumptions that end up not being effective at all.

When teachers are making instructional decisions, especially on the fly, it involves three components that taken together tell a story about a child in a certain moment of time—(1) what data the teacher has that describes most recent information about what a child knows (summative test scores over time, recent test scores both formative and summative), (2) the teacher's professional judgment about that child's learning environment (what's going on at school such as special education needs, what triggers a child has for challenges in behavior, knowledge of cognitive and behavioral deficiencies that hinder learning), and; (3) their personal knowledge and relationship with that child (child's home life, personality traits, and a teacher's attitudes toward child).

Teachers use these three components throughout the day for on-their-feet decisions about instruction during the lesson as well as for overall lesson planning. These components are in play as teachers make decisions about learning objectives, the type of activities that will form learning experiences, selection of tools and resources used in learning experiences, and assessment strategies that will reveal how well students are learning. As complex as those three components are, this is the fundamental work of teachers. The complexity of these decisions and their implementation is why teaching is not a babysitting service, but a profession that requires ongoing training and attention to practice.

As difficult and arduous using the three components named above may be, a fourth component is needed in education when teachers are making instructional decisions. Knowledge of the education research that underlies the complex decisions that the teacher makes. This impacts a teacher's actions by making them more effective and invariably results in better student learning. You might say that teachers learn that in undergraduate or graduate courses.

If so, why do we forget this after the teacher leaves those hallways and begins to apply theories and research in practice?

Research is the careful consideration of study regarding a particular concern or problem using scientific methods. According to the American sociologist Earl Robert Babbie, "research is a systematic inquiry to describe, explain, predict, and control the observed phenomenon." It begins with a question or problem and follows a scientific process to find answers. Good research is replicable, reproducible, and transparent.

There are educational research studies that have been validated over time yet still not used often enough. For example, there are many studies related to *wait time*. Wait time studies establish that the average student needs at least three to five seconds of wait time after a question has been asked to process the question and provide an answer; challenged students need at least ten seconds. Yet the average wait time in the hundreds of classrooms around the country averages—wait for it—one second. When wait time and feedback are practiced regularly, students can learn more effectively.

But not all research is equal. Educators can make better instructional decisions if they engage less with conflicting and incomplete studies and be more thoughtful and discerning about robust bodies of research, particularly metanalysis studies that look at what is common across many studies. How often have we heard the phrase "theory into practice"? It is an overused term in education jargon to mean take what we know works and apply it in the classroom. So why do we rarely see it as consistent practice or topic of conversation at collegial meetings?

One solution is to encourage *adapting scientific evidence for use in education and application in the classroom a core activity of teachers. This can be accomplished in a variety of ways: professional learning communities, ongoing conversations in planning meetings; topics of concentration in professional development; or even selection of graduate courses. But when do teachers have the time for all that? The answer is that educators cannot afford to not* have the time. The reorganization of teachers' time is needed to prioritize adding this fourth component and administrators can make that happen.

Let's get back to the idea of data. Data in and of itself is inert. It has no meaning, no value until assigned one. In a data-driven education world, it seems that all data is important and must be assigned value. When all data is assigned equal value, it makes it even more difficult for teachers to discern what is important in their decision making. Data should help teachers solve problems. It should help answer questions teachers need answers to when making instructional decisions for individual students, as well as whole classes. In many schools there are data walls, plotting individual student data by grade levels, standardized measures, and other groupings. These give a needed visual representation of where a student places in regard to their peers but only within the context of whatever testing system is being used.

Limiting data to only one use puts teachers at a disadvantage. Looking at data from differing testing systems measuring for the same objective is much richer information for a teacher. The timelines for these data usually are by semester, grading period, or the school year. But what about using data beyond one time period? How often do teachers look at, or even have access to, a student's data story over time, over many grade levels?

When looking at data, when being told about data, when talking about data, teachers can augment their knowledge of data by collecting data themselves. This harkens back to the action research mentioned in chapter 2. When teachers make a practice of collecting their own data, analyzing that data in their classrooms, and evaluating the application of the data, they become more knowledgeable about what questions to ask of administrators, outside consultants, and their colleagues. Firsthand knowledge of "what works" bestows more professionalism to teachers and provide a stronger foundation for effective teaching.

Another extremely effective practice a teacher can have is to always ask why. Why was it taught this way instead of that way? Why did that student respond in that way? Why did the teacher use this strategy over another strategy? Often when teachers are asked why they did something such as choosing one instructional or management strategy over another they simply do not have an answer. Maybe it was intuition, but actions are often made on assumption. Assumptions that they anticipated what would happen, but when confronted with the fact that it didn't happen, teachers get frustrated and often blame the student.

For example, during the planning process, the teacher makes an assumption about how quickly students will learn a new concept. However, during the lesson, students do not grasp it. Teachers often will continue using the same strategy, frustrating herself and her students rather than switching to another tactic. An egregious example is when teachers expect students to perform certain tasks such as return homework assignments. But when the homework is not returned as expected, students are called "lazy." If a teacher asks why she may be able to uncover the reasons she or he used that demeaning term.

As noted above, a teacher should ask why he or she is doing something. Next, a teacher should ask how. If I know the learning goals, how can they be accomplished in my classroom? What will it look like when the goals are successful? What will the student's answer, work, responses look like when he or she learned it? What does the term "learned" mean? Is it the ability to recall? to paraphrase? Or does a teacher hope for a deeper level of knowing?

The "why" question is the problem the teacher needs to solve. The "how" question can be found in the research. A good place to start is by defining anecdote in research methodology, knowing the difference between correlation and causation, determining how social research differs from medical research, knowing how generalizing works, and other core elements of research 101. Become versed in these concepts so a regular, consistent practice in the classroom can be established.

It also moves the planning process from being activity-based to being learning-based. For example, completing a worksheet, reading pages from a text, or playing a game are activities. But a teacher needs the education research context and knowledge to determine if these activities meet the learning goal.

Being able to distinguish science from pseudoscience as a habit of mind should be part of every teacher's knowledge base. It is a good starting place for determining what works and what does not work in the classroom. For example, science will have the following characteristics: it may change with new evidence, it is subjected with ruthless peer review, and it takes account of all new discoveries. Science invites criticism includes verifiable results and accurate measurement, and it limits claims of usefulness.

Pseudoscience, on the other hand, relies on fixed ideas, has no peer review, and selects only favorable discoveries. Pseudoscience sees criticism as conspiracy, relies on nonrepeatable results, makes claims of widespread usefulness, and relies on "ball park" measurement. Delineating between correlation and causation also will help separate the two. A correlation between two variables doesn't always mean one causes the other. A famous and humorous illustration of this concept states that global warming increased since the late 1800s and pirate numbers decreased, therefore lack of pirates did not cause global warming.

Remembering our history in education, what worked in the past, what bandwagons we jumped on that didn't pan out, is all part of teacher as researcher. Phrases such as "evidence based," "best practices," "research based" are thrown around especially by those others outside of the classroom. This is as if there is an inherent understanding of what these phrases mean and how they apply in the classroom. But the education community, especially teachers, should always examine the role of evidence in their practice.

Research in "what works best" should be embedded as seamlessly as possible into the everyday work of lesson planning, team meetings, faculty meetings, lesson delivery. In fact, teachers should drive the research agenda by identifying questions that need to be answered. Research resources be they texts, outside experts, or other materials, should be made available to teachers, enabling them to be critical and thoughtful consumers of evidence. This empowers teachers to make independent, informed decisions about what works by not only consuming, but also by generating good quality evidence and using it thoughtfully.

Teachers are not statisticians or pure researchers. But they should be familiar with the basics of research and the science of teaching and learning. Where to start? By establishing as an integrated part of the school culture, the ability of the teachers to ask, discuss, and collaborate with each other to answer these questions.

1. What is the problem or question that will be investigated?
2. Is the question about diagnosis (Why does the problem exist?), impact (Does a particular strategy "work"?), or implementation (What needs to be in place for the strategy to work?)?
3. What are the methods used to investigate? Is it qualitative or quantitative which will inform the methods?
4. What does it mean to establish validity? Of a particular research study?
5. What does reliability mean in research?
6. What about credibility as it pertains to qualitative studies?
7. What are the results of the study? What does statistical significance mean in reference to a quantitative study?
8. What are the practical implications of the results of the study? How are the results relevant to professional experience?

Most solid research articles follow a similar design. They begin with the question or problem to be investigated, some background literature, a review of the sample and data collection process, and end with a discussion. When teachers are informed consumers of research, they have important new ideas to apply in the classroom.

Most teachers are not averse to research. But it can be overwhelming and gets lost in the day-to-day lesson preparation and teaching. Remember the arc of the school year: teachers go from high enthusiasm and excitement at beginning of year to survival mode during testing season to puttering out from exhaustion at end of year.

Teachers receive instruction in Research 101 in undergraduate and graduate school. But without practice, those skills fall away and get buried in all the teaching minutia. Sometimes in graduate school, those skills are put into use for a thesis or dissertation, but rarely do teachers have a chance to conduct research in a thoughtful and consistent way once they are in the classroom. Action research can be used as an approach to keep research skills fresh and provide practical applications as well as new knowledge to a teacher's practice.

Should teachers be expected to do a dissertation level research every year they teach? Of course not. But there are ways for administrators to help teachers sort through the sheer volume of research already in the public domain. Additionally, administrators can certainly provide teachers with resources to conduct their own action research on a consistent basis. Be aware when new valid research is presented which may refute older research, there will be a need to discuss why and how it may affect teachers. Administrators can provide strategies for teachers to share their new knowledge with each other. Of course, this means prioritizing how teachers use their time.

Laying a firm foundation of education research knowledge will enable teachers to move to planning and delivering instruction on a sure and proven path. No longer will teachers rely on assumptions, intuition, or gut feelings as sole arbitrator of how to teach. In the next chapter, teachers will learn a simple strategy for collecting information process data while he or she is teaching. A simple enough strategy for checking for understanding that is not practiced enough in todays' classrooms. But a powerful strategy that can make a dramatic, positive change in student learning.

PRACTICAL MATTERS

1. Teachers and administrators should review basic research principles as an ongoing, deliberate agenda item in faculty meetings, planning meetings, and Professional Learning Communities. Conducting a semantics exercise such as vocabulary squares will help clarify terms and get everyone on the same page. The research terms can become a natural part of professional conversations to determine what questions to ask vendors and consultants. No vendor should be able to sell a product to schools without the scrutiny and input of teachers.

2. Both teachers and administrators should become more transparent and respectful about their own values and understand how they may differ from scientific evidence. Schools are political creations, and community and personal values are a natural part of the culture. There will be issues teachers will not agree on—and well-intentioned people can disagree on issues—so we must put them on the table so that discussions about scientific merit of findings do not turn into "cloaked discussions of values." This can only confuse the conversation and lead to distrust among all who work at a school.

3. Teachers can keep reflective note entries in a journal, science notebook, or lesson plan book. These notes can address questions or problems that come up on a regular basis that they might want to investigate. Share these with colleagues and develop a plan for supporting each other in the action research process and filtering research studies for relevant information.

4. Administrators should prioritize research as a foundation in making effective instructional decisions. Remember studies already exist in the public domain and action research can be done in the teachers' own classrooms. Support this priority in the form of providing resources such as outside experts who can review processes for teachers' action plans, time in the school day to converse, plan, and support each other in these pursuits, and participating themselves in an action research project.

4

How Is Learning Assessed During Teaching?

Philip Done, a third-grade teacher, wrote a delightful book called *32 Third Graders and One Class Bunny: Life Lessons from Teaching*. Done mixes humor and wisdom in a collection of essays about his experiences. In the telling of everyday happenings in his classroom—nervous first day of school, Halloween parades, zipping zippers that won't zip—he connects what happens in his classroom to all of our experiences in teaching regardless of the age of our students.

One of Done's essays hones in on a topic that resonates with the theme of this book, a simple concept that reveals many layers of complexity once analyzed. It's called *Teacher School*. After a student asks him why teachers always tell students to write in complete sentences Done replies that teachers learn that in teacher school and he regales the students with all the things teachers learn there. Things such as how to push a stapler, how to turn a jump rope, put stars on papers, and how to pull down a map.

The second year of teacher school brings lessons on how to unjam the copier and how to practice saying "Walk!" until you can say it really loud. Year Three teachers learn teacher jokes and in Year Four teachers have to take classes in Glaring at Children Who Play with Velcro During Storytime and "How to Say Now Get Back to Work."

Reading this essay at the beginning of professional development sessions reminds teachers of what they may or may not have learned in "Teacher School" and to ask what they still use today. For example, teachers all learned about assessment, both formative and summative, maybe even learned how to write test items and score them. But little of that stays with teachers when they hit the first year of teaching. Before moving into a discussion of the instructional design process, there must be a discussion about the most misunderstood, misused, and most ignored overarching instructional strategy—the foundation of formative assessment during the teaching process.

What if teachers were told there was a simple method to use in the classroom that would dramatically change student learning for the better? That it neither cost any money, nor had to be printed and handed out to students, nor require any extra forms or paperwork? Too good to be true? Actually, it's not. It is called *Checking for Understanding (CFU)*. Educators have probably heard of it because it is a formative assessment strategy that has had any number of books written about it along, together with a plethora of both scholarly and practical journal articles. Teacher evaluation checklists have included it with regularity.

These resources provide some valuable tools and some of the suggested strategies have made it into classrooms and into some practice. However, types of formative assessments that require additional time, effort, and resources by teachers such as entry and exit slips or quizzes and polls, seldom get used on a regular basis. Unless these assessments are embedded into everyday instruction and actually used to adjust instruction while the teacher is teaching, they rise and fall with the latest fad.

To make checking for understanding a daily practice, teachers can adopt and practice a foundational method that uses the data right in front of them while teaching. This is a method that is precise and enables a teacher to make instructional decisions on an individual, group, or whole class level in an instant. This method of collecting data guides the pacing of the lesson and allows students to clarify their own learning and the teacher to know without a doubt who is learning and who is not.

Most importantly, checking for understanding removes the assumption that students have learned new content and removes learning gaps for students. As all teachers know, these learning gaps happen and get compounded when some children move from grade to grade and fall further and further behind. Yet teachers have the power to make sure children do not fall through any cracks by changing their practice to include this level of checking for understanding whenever teaching new content.

What is this magic method, you ask? It is a method of asking key questions during whole group or small group instruction *while* teaching, assessing why a student may have answered incorrectly, and providing effective feedback. Many teachers likely say they already do this. However, evidence suggests this method is used rarely, if at all. Teachers make assumptions that students "know" what is taught and move on, but then in the final assessment, find out students did not know the material at all.

Teachers wonder what happened when the summative assessment reveals little to no learning. Teachers know what they taught and made an assumption students learned it. Thus forms a learning gap.

When teachers collect their own data in real time during teaching, a precise administration of the check for understanding method will vastly improve student learning. But using the method outlined below does not just happen. It must be built into the lesson design, practiced consistently, and continually perfected. It requires a change in how lessons are planned and taught. Remember: change is difficult.

Look at each step outlined below closely. Determine if you have any reservations or doubts about if or how they work. Remember that the bias you bring to the method will affect the implementation. Have someone, perhaps an instructional coach or trusted colleague, give authentic feedback to your lesson planning and practice. This feedback needs to happen on a regular basis. Have professional conversations around what works and what doesn't work.

Inevitably you have to change small behaviors to make larger changes. Teachers sometimes do not see what needs to be changed in the midst of teaching a lesson. However, when the teacher is collecting data as they teach, they can make decisions on the spot about whether something needs to be retaught, students need to be regrouped, or a step in a process has been left out.

Each step of this method is backed up by research and validated over time, sometimes going back decades. When you read the steps and the research behind it, most teachers will think, well, that makes perfect sense. So why aren't we doing this all the time? Why aren't we taught this method in undergraduate school? We will get to some of those answers as well as some of the caveats in the implementation towards the end of the chapter.

One of the most frustrating challenges in education is that teachers do not regularly use practices that have unassailable evidence fidelity to those practices that have an immediate, significant impact on student learning such as checking for understanding during a lesson. Fads, ideologies, personalities, and other barriers to using evidence-based practices regularly in the classroom are to blame. In spite of the millions of dollars spent each year on professional development, inferior practices are allowed to continue. This problem can be resolved by prioritizing evidence-based training. But this must be within the context that "less is more."

Schools take on too many initiatives that teachers are not allowed to pursue and practice with any depth, so success is not possible without a laser focus. Learning the principles of checking for understanding while teaching is an initiative that must be taken on and teachers must be allowed to "stick to it" until practiced in every classroom with fidelity.

For now, let's break down a strategy for checking for understanding into six steps—six steps performed sequentially that can be put into practice right away. Not perfected right away but with constant use and modification these steps can become the foundation for teaching any content area, any age level, in any classroom.

STEP 1: *INSTRUCT*

The CFU (Checking for Understanding) method works best when providing direct instruction of *new* content to a whole class. Regardless of span of knowledge levels, age ranges, demographics of students, or type of curriculum, there is always a need to teach content. This is the second part of the learning objective. Fractions, civil war battles, prepositions. Once content is taught to the whole class, teachers can then use the data they collected during this step and begin to differentiate and target instruction. More on those strategies in next chapter.

STEP 2: *ASK A SPECIFIC QUESTION*

Teachers ask a lot of questions all day. Differentiating types of questions is an important skill for teachers. Some questions are classroom management questions but most are academic questions. In the lesson planning, the teacher would have identified the key points of the content that she wants to make sure students "get." And she would have developed specific questions to ask during the delivery of the lesson. Specific questions related to the content explain, demonstrate, or illustrate overall concepts that were taught in the lesson. Questions such as such as "What is one half of 50?" or "What is the first stage in the metamorphosis of the caterpillar?"

If the question is a rote answer or a yes or no question, the teacher can increase the level of the question by asking students why they chose the answer, whether or not the answer is correct. Establishing how the student's mind works enables the teacher to analyze why students make mistakes while at the same time increasing critical thinking skills for students. More information about the teacher's feedback after specific questions are answered by students will be addressed in Step 6.

Each question is asked not to a particular student, but to the whole class so all of them can begin to formulate an answer in their minds. The one question NOT to ask is "Are there any questions?" Most teachers get blank stares when this is asked because students find it embarrassing to ask questions in front of their peers and/or genuinely do not know what question to ask. In addition, the teacher cannot get precise information from individual students as to whether or not they learned the material.

STEP 3: *MAKE TIME TO WAIT FOR A RESPONSE*

Wait time—it's been around for decades and has been validated many times in the research as important to learning. Once a teacher asks a key question, the teacher should wait at least three seconds. Some students may need up to ten seconds. This is where the teacher's knowledge of his or her students come into play. The teacher may differentiate the wait time to accommodate students learning needs.

Sometimes a variation of wait time called "think pair share" is used. Students turn to a partner and ask each other the question before responding to the teacher. The teacher will need to give a time limit and use an attention signal to return the focus to him or her. When beginning this "think pair" share method with students, let students practice the process of talking to each, sticking to the question, and ending their conversation when the teacher uses the attention signal. Students are so used to being told to be quiet they may have a hard time talking to each other in the middle of a lesson.

Of course, the teacher will also need an attention signal to bring students' focus back to the whole class. Elementary teachers use an attention signal regularly for classroom management such as clapping to a rhyme such as "1–2–3 eyes on me!" Middle and high school students sometimes use the school mascot or cheer as an attention signal. They all have the same purpose—to signal the end of think pair sharing and focus back on the whole class.

The tone the teacher sets in the classroom can enable or hinder this method. Teachers can give students permission to talk during this strategy and help them understand why it is important to think aloud with a peer. While teachers are being metacognitive, they can also help students be metacognitive. Explain wait time to students and practice it relentlessly. The students will recognize the benefit right away.

As proven as the wait time method is, the average wait time observed in hundreds of classrooms is *one* second. Wait time is a difficult skill for teachers to master. It must be practiced over and over. Teachers must come up with ways to help themselves such as using a counting method in their heads after they ask a question. For example, one Mississippi, two Mississippi, three Mississippi.

Another tactic to practice wait time is for teachers to pace five steps one way and five steps in another to avoid rushing into seeking an answer. If there are challenged students in the room—non-English speakers, special education students, or slow learners—then waiting 10 seconds is a must-do.

For many teachers, this feels like it takes too long because it takes time away from moving ahead. It does feel awkward in the beginning because it is a change. But this change will make a big impact on student learning. Again, students must be taught not to shout out an answer, must be taught that everyone is thinking of an answer in his or her minds, and that everyone will have an equal opportunity to give an answer aloud. But the teacher realizes the necessity of giving wait time and it becomes a consistent classroom practice, student learning improves.

STEP 4: *CHOOSE A NONVOLUNTEER*

In most classrooms, when a teacher asks a question, hands go up in the air. Some students are so eager to answer a question that they squirm in their seats to get the teacher's attention or wave their hands frantically. A lot of the time it is the same hands that go up for most of the questions. Quite often students shout out answers without raising their hands, despite admonitions to the contrary. Oftentimes this is allowed by the teacher, contrary to their rule of not shouting out. This inconsistency can make classroom management challenging.

When teachers call on students with their hands raised, they are calling on *volunteers*. These are the students that validate the teaching, that confirm that those particular students are learning, even if it is only the same two or three doing all the answering. But what about the other students in the class? Are they learning as well? How does a teacher check if these other students are learning?

The best way is to call on *nonvolunteers*—students chosen at random from the classroom. A teacher can tell students that he is taking volunteers for responses or that he only calls on nonvolunteers. Teachers can support student learning further when they explain the processes, procedures, and the reasons why. If this is a new procedure in the classroom, students will even remind you when told how this method improves their learning.

There are many methods of choosing a random student. The most popular one is to use Popsicle sticks or tongue depressors with student names written on them and then choose one at random from a container. But the teacher can also assign a number to each child and use a random number generator application on a device although this is less personal. This type of selection is also built into digital devices such as the response clickers that accompany interactive whiteboards.

The point is that the student you call on is truly random and students know it is random. Some teachers *think* they are calling on random students but oftentimes it is a classroom management decision. For example, calling on a student a teacher think may not be paying attention. This may be a valid decision, but a teacher should know *when* he or she is doing it and *why* he or she did it. (Of course, this also perpetuates the myth that teachers have eyes in the back of their heads because they see all, a myth we might want to continue.)

Sometimes teachers look at a class list and choose a student. That is not a random choice, particularly if the teacher already had someone in mind or is using the class list as a prop to call on an inattentive student. Students are able to uncannily pick up the teacher's motive, no matter the students' ages: it is futile to try and "trick" them. The key is that the students have to know it is truly random so that all will pay attention and think of an answer when a question is asked and wait time is given.

If a student anticipates being called on, they can be better prepared. Does this mean you don't call on volunteers occasionally? Or call on students for classroom management reasons? Of course not. The teacher needs to make the best decisions at the time of a lesson. But a teacher knowing why, when, and how he or she calls on students during a whole class lesson gives more power to those instructional decisions.

Another way of checking for answers is to have every student use a whiteboard to write down an answer. Sometimes this is used in combination with think pair sharing where individuals write down an answer or in pairs. The whiteboard can be as simple as a sheet of blank paper in a plastic sheet protector or fancy ones sold in teacher supply catalogs. The teacher can give a signal and all students hold boards up and the teacher can make a quick glance around the room to see what students wrote down. Teachers can then use a random selection process to call on students to read their answers. This method gives the teacher some data to determine if a majority of the students are on the same page with her.

If the response involves a process such as a mathematical equation, teachers can get a look at how the students are thinking from the whiteboard and make decisions to reteach or regroup later. For example, an algebra teacher had students show steps to solving an equation on a whiteboard after teaching the steps. Many students were solving the equation wrong and the teacher assumed students were making errors in a later step. But the whiteboards showed him it was an earlier step—quite a surprise to him. He then retaught that step and connected it to the other steps.

When a teacher clearly designates whether volunteers or nonvolunteers should answer questions, he or she can avoid the trap that teachers often get into. The trap of allowing students to shout out answers. This can serve a purpose if volunteers are called on and the teacher gives permission. If students are answering as one class, this is a choral response. It is more of an engagement strategy to get students' attention and focus on a question.

The line is murky here as to whether choral response is a classroom management technique or an instructional strategy. It leans toward being a motivation strategy because the teacher cannot know what each student is answering individually. If it is a non-key question, then a teacher may choose this strategy. But if it is a key question, this works the same way the raising of hands. A few students are loud and vocal, the quiet ones sit back and do not participate.

Providing clarity to the students as to the procedures for who will answer questions will translate into a more trusting relationship between teachers and students. There are no "gotchas" and each student can be held accountable for their own learning.

STEP 5: *LISTEN TO THE RESPONSE*

Truly listening takes some slowing down, which is difficult to do as practicing wait time. Listening at this step involves paying attention to nuances in a child's answer as well as what the teacher knows about this particular child in this particular learning environment. Understanding these nuances will inform the type of feedback the teacher will give. Nuances to listen out for are: (1) hesitancy, or (2) confusion.

The teacher must determine if the hesitancy and/or confusion is a matter of not having heard or not understanding the question. The teacher can then either provide a prompt, restate the question, or reword the question. The teacher knows if the student called on has special needs and can tailor accordingly. The goal is not to embarrass or shame a child for not knowing but to provide support for ensuring success for the child.

When practiced consistently, this CFU method can make all children successful in their responses regardless of their cognitive ability or special learning needs. The next step can ensure the teacher makes that happen.

STEP 6: *RESPOND EFFECTIVELY USING RANDOM SAMPLING*

A student has made a response and the teacher has provided a prompt or reworded the question. However, the answer is still wrong. At this important moment, one of the most powerful strategies an educator can use is to tell that student he will come back to him. And mean it! The teacher moves to another student. This next student answers correctly. The teacher echoes that student's correct answer. The teacher calls on a third student. This student answers correctly. The teacher again echoes the correct answer. And so on.

The student that answered incorrectly has now heard the correct answer at least eight times. The teacher returns to the original student. Repeat the question. Students may answer correctly at this point or you may tell them the answer directly and have them repeat it. Sometimes a student is partially correct, and the teacher simply needs to elaborate on the answer. Other times a student is incorrect and a teacher needs to explain the answer before moving on to the next student response.

The power of this method is that *no student is allowed to not know the answer*! Oftentimes a student answers incorrectly and the teacher moves on to the next student without ever going back to the original student that answered incorrectly. When the student then gets the answer incorrect on a summative test, teachers are surprised, having made the dreaded assumption that the student heard the correct answer later and processed it in his or her brain. This CFU method allows a more precise strategy of not letting any children fall through any "cracks" in the lesson.

The above-mentioned example used the technique of echoing the correct answer. This method comes from brain research that says when the correct answer is repeated multiple times, our brains can put the new information from short-term to long-term memory. Asking several students the same question and echoing the answer provides this opportunity. This is also an opportunity for teachers to take a random sampling during a lesson. If one out of three students misses an answer, the teacher can determine it is a problem with an individual student.

However, if two out of three students miss an answer in random sampling, this may indicate that a skill or concept needs to be retaught. It is better to find out immediately than find out on a later quiz that the student did not know. By then teachers have moved on to the next lesson. Again, that's how children form gaps in their learning.

How and when a teacher uses this CFU method and how effectively she gives feedback, will have an impact on the pacing of the lesson. If a lesson has moved too quickly and the students have not caught on, this should inform the teacher that the current lesson needs redoing and the next lesson will need revision to accommodate the change. Sometimes the teacher overestimates or underestimates how quickly some students learn a new skill or concept. It goes without saying that this can change from year to year and lesson to lesson depending on the makeup of the students in the classroom.

The steps outlined above let the teacher know who knows what while the lesson is being taught. That is important data that should inform teachers' decisions about what steps are next.

Some of the misgivings heard from teachers about using this method include the following:

1. This method takes too much time.

Teachers are constantly pushed for time. It is a trap educators must not let themselves fall into because it leads to assumptions about what, how, and when students are learning. It does take more time in the beginning because students are new to the procedures and processes. They must unlearn their usual response of waving their hands or shouting out answers. But this procedure can be similar to the procedures teachers put into place to organize their classrooms such as where to put completed work, how papers are collected, and so on.

Processes and procedures are used daily, mainly for classroom management. This CFU process is used to improve student learning. As teachers practice, they will get better at discerning what questions are key, when to call on volunteers, and when to allow choral responses. The students will pick up on the process even earlier, calling teachers out if they skip a step. The trust established between teacher and student in ensuring students know they are not allowed to *not* learn is priceless.

2. Random sampling techniques are scary and anxiety producing for some students.

Especially for special education students, random sampling techniques cause a good bit of anxiety. For these students, it likely is a good idea to pull them aside and tell them what will be happening. Teachers can manipulate the stick pulling to accommodate these students but it must be only as a specific solution for a specific student. If other students catch on that this happening, all the trust you have established can go down the drain. The same is true if teachers want to make sure a specific student is called on for a specific question and the teacher "fake" calls a name. Trust is a fragile commodity and teachers must make these instructional decisions with an understanding what unintended consequences may occur.

3. So much to cover, so little time.

The trick here is to take time when beginning using this method to differentiate between the types of questions when the questions are asked during the lesson. Key questions must be front loaded into the lesson plan. But often teachers think of questions on the spot depending on how students are responding to the new content. Shouldn't educators ask those? Of course! As the instructional leader, only the teacher knows his or her classroom's dynamic.

Questioning should be intentional and meaningful. Wait time, as well as the effectiveness of random sampling, has been validated over many decades as a valuable strategy for improving student learning. It's not just a new activity in a lesson—it is an ongoing pedagogical strategy to be used across content areas and grade levels.

Practice and figure out how to slow down. It saves time later because a teacher will know at the time of teaching if a concept needs to be retaught rather than waiting until after a test has been given to find out students did not understand the new material. This creates a backlog of what needs to get retaught. In the end, this usually never happens because an educator must invariably move on to the next standard.

4. This method seems effective but the entire process day in and day out seems too robotic and boring for students.

The teacher sets the tone in the classroom. If students are bored with the method, then the teacher is probably giving off those "vibes." Students line up every day to go to lunch or change classes. Are they bored? Maybe. But they are also excited for the next activity. When teachers make it exciting for students to learn new content and show proof of that learning during a lesson, students are motivated to continue the practice. Again, the teacher has to be discerning about which lessons and which parts of a lesson to use this method. The method loses that power when it is used for procedural reasons rather than instructional. For example, lining children up or giving children helper roles. Save it for key questions during the teaching of new material.

Collecting data during the questioning, keeping an eye on classroom behavior, and making decisions about next steps in the lesson, all while teaching a lesson in front of students is difficult. This is why teachers are professionals at their jobs, requiring undergraduate training and ongoing professional development. It's also why teachers are so tired at the end of the day. A lot of brain work happens in the classroom—from students and teachers! But items discussed in this chapter are vital to a vibrant learning environment and to help educators ensure success for students and themselves.

PRACTICAL MATTERS

1. This CFU method, when used across a school, by all teachers, can send a powerful message to students. Students should not be able to be alert in some classes because they may be called on and sit disengaged in another because the teacher only calls on those with their hands raised. Students know what they can "get away" with from all their teachers. This is not a nefarious intent, but rather because that is the human response for their age, particularly if a subject is hard for them or they are uninterested. Students scope out teachers on day one and decide which ones they respect and which ones they do not.

Administrators can lead and nurture an evidence-based culture in their schools by choosing only one or two initiatives such as checking for understanding while teaching and using wait time. Emphasizing only these two initiatives, monitoring them on a regular basis in every classroom will result in dramatic changes in student learning. Focusing on a whole faculty approach is necessary for success.

The adage about being "mean" the first weeks of school versus being "too nice," may be bad advice. At the heart of the teaching profession, is the steadfast truth that students want to learn, that they need routines and structure in their learning, that they want to trust their teachers to make sure they do learn. It is possible to be firm, fair, and consistent without being "mean."

2. *Eliminate "coming to the board" as a method for students to display learning.* Having students use whiteboards is a lot more efficient for a teacher to find out if students are understanding new content. When two, three, or four or more students come to the board—usually to perform a mathematics problem—the teacher can only determine if those students can perform the task. To know whether all the students in the classroom can perform the task, all students would need to come to the board in groups or at the same time. This is a highly inefficient way for the teacher to collect data.

3. *Administrators can put an emphasis on this method at the beginning of the year by making time for professional conversation about teachers' beliefs and assumptions about checking for understanding.* This can be an intentional strategy during faculty meetings, professional learning community goals, professional book club selections, or coaching sessions. Again, a semantics activity such as vocabulary squares can enable teachers and administrators to determine what barriers may be in place to prevent successful implementation.

4. *Emphasize only one or two change goals for the year.* These goals should be integrated with classroom observation checklists, faculty meeting agendas, and professional development activities. In fact, teachers themselves should agree as a faculty what those goals are and support each other in their implementation. This is how a positive culture is created.

Adopt a "less is more" attitude so teachers can go in depth on a topic and apply sustained focus on making a positive change. Enable teachers to practice new skills such as CFU in training sessions that are coached by their colleagues or outside experts until that skill is mastered. Feedback should be focused not on individuals but whole school faculty needs.

When observations, especially, are targeted for a specific teaching behavior, teachers get more comfortable with observations and begin to let go of the evaluative tone that makes teachers and observers adversaries rather than partners. Allowing time for peer observations and feedback furthers this culture shift. Teachers can feel supported and can begin to make changes in their practice early on and refine it throughout the year.

Oftentimes teachers want a "grade" and they want to know how well they performed after an observation as if it were a summative assessment. Giving constructive feedback and having professional dialogue can go a long way to instill trust between teachers and observers with follow-up plans made on a consistent basis. Making observations on a formative assessment with the collaborative goal of improving teaching practice is a major shift for school cultures but one that benefits all.

5. *Clear up semantics around "formative assessment" so everyone has same the understanding of the meaning of the word and its translation into practice.* Differentiate between data received from students from achievement data such as standardized tests, benchmark tests, unit tests, and chapter tests and instructional process data. Data received from achievement tests is called summative data. This data is not received until after a student has been taught a lesson and, in some cases, not received for many months in the case of standardized tests.

Instructional process data is a result of formative assessment that takes place during the teaching. This is data teachers keep in their head, for the most part, and use to make decisions about monitoring and adjusting the teaching based on student responses. Achievement tests result in assessment *of* learning. Formative assessments result in assessment *for* learning. Each have a role for teachers as instructional leaders. Professional conversations around how to use each in decision-making for student learning need to be ongoing on a weekly, if not, daily basis.

Other professional conversations must also involve the types of checking for understanding, how they are practiced, and their effectiveness in assessing student learning. For example, many teachers use a "thumbs up" or "thumbs down" method of assessment. This method may be effective in certain situations and teachers can clarify when it may be useful and when it may not. Another example is the use of "exit slips." When should these be used as a formative assessment method? If the teacher needs to make decisions about who is ready for independent work before assigning homework, it may not be effective. But in other teaching situations it may well be.

A Google search for formative assessment will result in a plethora of activities such as creating mind maps, creating a KWL chart, using color cards for students to let teachers know if they need help, writing a fake Twitter post, or conducting a classroom TED talk. There are also numerous professional books devoted to the subject. Teachers can be overwhelmed but must do the necessary work of evaluating each method as to its effectiveness and usefulness for teacher decision-making while teaching.

The most important question for teachers to ask in this evaluation is if they will receive the information on student learning in time to adjust teaching strategies and/or make decisions about if a student is ready for independent work. A good place to start is listing as a faculty all the methods currently being used. It may be hard for teachers to let go of some methods. But if those methods are not supported by data from the education research field or the teacher's own data, they must be eliminated. Until it is discussed in depth, teachers will continue to use ineffective practices.

6. Evaluate which technology tools should be used for formative assessment while teaching. There are many technology tools and software available for teachers to use for formative assessment such as student response systems that accompany interactive whiteboards and software such as Kaboom. Just because they are available does not mean they will meet the needs of the teacher to gauge student learning.

This evaluation of technology tools becomes paramount in virtual teaching and learning. There are some tools built into synchronous platforms such as yes and no buttons and private chat features that allow a teacher to know what a student knows and does not know in real time. In a virtual teaching setting, a teacher must be keenly aware of the different skill set needed to teach in this medium. That knowledge must extend to what formative assessment methods are effective.

Sometimes the set-up of the tool is complex and takes more time than another simpler method. Choosing the appropriate technology is an important skill for teachers. There is more about this topic in chapter 7. When teachers are knowledgeable about formative assessment research, they will be able to choose among the tools that are evidence-based and know why he or she is integrating it into instruction.

7. When the practice of not assigning student independent work before the teacher has been assured the student has learned the new content has become consistent, it will be time to have a faculty discussion about the effectiveness of assigning homework. Assigning any independent work to be completed by a student outside of class is an entrenched practice and will be a difficult conversation for a faculty to engage in.

Oftentimes, especially at the middle and high school levels, students do not complete their homework for various reasons. A main reason, however, is that they did not understand how to complete the work. This happens when teachers release them from a lesson without checking for understanding on an individual basis. A major amount of time is spent the next school day on collecting homework, grading homework, and "going over" homework. If this is familiar to teachers, a conversation is needed about whether this as a practice that constitutes malpractice and how it can be either eliminated or redesigned to meet the learning needs of students.

8. *Conduct a school-wide inventory and analysis of kinds of questions teachers ask students in the course of a day.* Invite teachers to visit each other's classes during a lesson and write down all the questions a teacher asks. It is not necessary to include the teacher's name. Once this survey is completed in several, if not all classrooms, teachers can sort all the questions into the following categories:

- Classroom management questions that keep the classroom operations moving.
- Rhetorical questions that emphasize a point or reinforce an idea.
- Closed questions that include factual questions that require students to recall specific information.
- Open questions that are used to promote discussion or student interaction.
- Probing questions that require students to go beyond the first question.
- Divergent questions that have no right or wrong answer.
- Higher order questions that require students to figure out answers rather than remember them.
- Affective questions that elicit expressions of attitudes, values, or feelings of students.
- Other types of questions not listed here.

Research on the questions teachers ask shows that about 60% require only recall of facts, 20% require students to think, and 20% are procedural in nature. How does the school surveyed compare with this research finding? If teachers conclude more thinking questions need to be asked of students, how will the teachers make that happen? How will administrators and instructional coaches support their goals?

5

How Is Effective Instruction Designed?

Chefs know about mirepoix. It is the "holy trinity" of carrots, onions, and celery that make up a powerful culinary combination that provides flavor and aroma to many basic dishes such as sauces, soups, and stocks. Various differences may occur such as measurements of each ingredient, the level of dicing, and even substitutions for the three main ingredients such as leeks for onions. These variances may result in different tasting dishes but, when applied using the same "chemistry," almost always results in something delicious to eat.

Teachers also know a "holy trinity" of sorts. It is taught in Education 101 and known as CIA: Curriculum, Instruction, and Assessment. If you picture a Venn diagram with CIA as the major circles, the center would be pedagogy—interactions between teachers, students, and the learning environment and the learning tasks. This is where it all comes together. The key to those interactions and strategies resides with the teacher—the instructional leader in the classroom—and the decisions she makes about the who, when, where, and why of those interactions.

While pedagogy is steeped in CIA and, in fact, does not exist without some combination of these three mains "ingredients," teachers, like chefs, vary on how they use CIA to design and deliver instructional strategies. Sometimes those decisions are made strategically but just as often, if not more so, those decisions become mechanical, guided by intuition. Sometimes false beliefs about what works. Add to the recipe experience and gut instinct. When all those ingredients are thrown together without much thought to the "chemistry," student learning—the major goal—can be hit or miss.

Most people have attended a school for twelve years and some have their own children in school. Therefore, everyone has an opinion about school. Individuals bring these experiences with them in the form of attitudes—good, bad, indifferent—to parent conference meetings, voting booths, and even policy making. If a parent had a negative experience with schooling, that attitude can be passed down to his or her children and that attitude plays itself out in different parenting behaviors. These experiences and opinions can drive policy when politicians campaigning on different platforms introduce new ideas into education policy or bring back ideas from the past.

Sometimes these policy initiatives have unintended consequences—especially for teachers. For example, over the last few decades, teachers have been subject to various types of evaluation in the form of classroom observations, observation checklists, new teacher induction activities, and recent attempts to tie these evaluation activities to teacher pay. These evaluative efforts all have an intended purpose of either helping teachers become better at their job or weeding out incompetent teachers.

The underlying purpose of these evaluations has really been to "fix" teachers as if they are broken down cars. With the "fix" comes various solutions from the "outside," but hardly any ever take into account what the teachers suggest. Top-down solutions usually encompass some type of training, or maybe some type of coaching, or new resources. These outside forces have a major effect on what happens in classrooms and how teachers respond affect whatever solutions are put in place.

Whatever solution is presented however, will come up short because the training, coaching, and resources likely will not be enough to sustain the "fix" over the long haul. Goal setting and bench marking are dictated by the school year, the testing calendar, and other sacred cows of education. This creates a toxic stew in the hunt for a "fix." This revolving door of policy making by politicians and ineffective translation of those policies into practice needs have not had the intended outcomes.

Even technology impacts accountability practices. Media formats have made everything more transparent, and while one might think this is a positive, omnipresent technology delivers unintended consequences. Teachers have come under fire. They are the face of education and a convenient scapegoat when things go awry. Collectively, teachers bear the brunt of complaints on social media about society's ills such as poverty, lack of funding in education, and other inequities.

With all the doom and gloom, it is no wonder teachers leave the profession in droves and feel more and more powerless in their profession. But what happens in schools and classrooms does not happen in a vacuum. There are pressures that teachers cannot control at all. Some pressures they may use their voice to alleviate. Some they may choose to confront.

However, there is one aspect of teaching that teachers have complete control over—instructional decisions and how they are delivered in the classroom. Within this context, a teacher makes all of the decisions and maintains his place as the instructional leader in the classroom. Many teachers think they have ceded this aspect over to the program gods, but indeed they have not.

There may be an edict from the district office that a certain program must be used twice a week, or that a resource must be used for certain students, or that a specific process must be used to address a narrow problem. Overall, however, the teacher decides how content is to be taught, what pedagogical practices will be used, and what his or her response will be during and after learning takes place.

In other words, *teachers are the instructional leaders in the classroom, and their power resides in that one powerful concept.* The choices teachers make in this crucial element of teaching will make or break whether students learn or not. These choices are that important. Reversing the mindset that says a teacher is powerless into one that makes a teacher believe in his or her awesome power can be the one cultural change that will make a difference in students' lives.

The power resides in the instructional decisions teachers make before, during, and after instruction. These decisions are those made during the planning phase, the teaching phase, and the reflection phase. All these phases are the design of the instruction. Determining what needs to be taught, how it will be taught, deciding key questions that drive checking for understanding as well as summative assessment, what will be the remediation methods for learning-challenged students and practice methods to maintain learning for the testing and beyond.

Designing instruction contains other considerations as well. For example, the intended audience, the intended outcome, resources to support instruction, and time frame. Teachers are expected to sort through these considerations and put them into a format called a lesson plan. And this process is always ongoing, with little to no time to reflect on and consider what needs to be done differently the next time.

Many teachers may have ideas once the lesson is over about what needs to change next time that lesson is taught. But then teachers must be on to the next lesson and the next. There is a pacing chart to consider and only 180 days to get it all done, minus days for unexpected events such as pep rallies, snow days, or medical emergencies.

The automaton nature of teaching, especially in the middle of the arc of the school year, can impede mindfulness of each days' lessons and render many thoughtful planning processes mechanical. For example, the speed at which teachers must constantly cycle through lessons is one explanation for why lesson planning has become a perfunctory activity. Again, the arc of the year and the waning of enthusiasm and excitement once the school year gets started have roles in this cycle as well.

Just as teachers are jaded about new programs that come along with a new administrator at the school or district level, so are they troubled about how to design instruction given the myriad of lesson planning resources available and the different lesson plan formats that come and go with new school level administrators. A plethora of digital sites offer resources and premade lesson plans. Even to veteran teachers, this can be overwhelming. Some administrators want lessons "turned in" weekly, some do not require them to be turned in at all. Although some administrators require plans to be posted by the door for visitors and others, often they pay no mind to them themselves during walk-throughs.

Unfortunately, sometimes the tail wags the dog. The resources available be they textbooks, a new program, or a new initiative drive how lessons are designed rather than the resources designed to fit the learning needs of students. Some programs have gone so far as to have scripted lessons that literally put words in teachers' mouths. It is no wonder teachers see the writing of a lesson plan as a mechanical effort rather than a strategic one.

What should go into lesson design? The important part of the design is the *process,* not just the actual final format for the lesson. As any designer knows, there must be some forethought put into a design before the final rendering. Brainstorming, sketches, conversation with colleagues and others, all with a foundation of "what works." It is a journey from curriculum standards to lesson plans, a journey fraught with misunderstandings, shortcuts, and sacrificing quality for speed.

Standards Based Education (SBE) began in the 1980s as a policy-based reform movement to establish what students should know and be able to do. It was designed to provide concrete standards by which each student could be measured and made its way in curriculum, assessments, and professional development. This movement led to the development of curriculum frameworks, later curriculum standards, that came to define the work of educators.

Curriculum standards establish general knowledge of what students should know and be able to accomplish academically. They are not learning objectives. These standards give guidelines for instructional content but do not help a teacher translate that into lesson plans. States and districts have developed pacing guides, suggested texts, and other resources usually created by a committee in the summer to help teachers translate the standards into a design for instruction.

Do these additional instructional aides help? Certainly, they do. But if the basic deconstruction of a standard and translation into a learning objective is misunderstood or made into a cut and paste activity, the lesson design goes off track quickly. One of the unintended and damaging consequences of SBE reform and the resulting accountability measures has been the mechanization of instructional planning and design.

Terms have developed around translating curriculum standards into instruction with the most popular being "unpacking" the standards. Usually this means a teacher must analyze the language of the standards to determine essential knowledge and skills. This activity has several steps that involve understanding the meaning of "essential" which then becomes developing "essential questions."

Many educators are also told they must prioritize the skills within the standards to determine power standards. However, power standards can be interpreted as selecting some parts of the standard that must be taught to the sacrifice of others. Each of the steps outlined in the unpacking process involves interpretation of terms and processes that get either watered down or misconstrued.

The best way to ensure the integrity of the standard is to break down that process into one important task: to establish learning objectives from the standards. Understanding how standards are written and then deconstructing a curriculum standard is the first step to establish learning objectives. If teachers do not do this rudimentary work first, learning becomes a lottery for students rather than a viable learning experience.

From a design perspective, the most important part of the beginning is *establishing the learning objective(s) for the lesson.* This seems so simple, but it is the beginning of total autonomy for the teacher as the instructional leader. This is also one of the holdovers from undergraduate training that gets twisted and turned into something else in the classroom.

Sometimes the learning objective is given other names such as TSWBAT: "the student will be able to." But that belies the nature of a learning objective. The learning objective must be defined by the teacher and is the basis for several decisions a teacher must make down the road. What will the students learn in this lesson that the teacher will be able to assess to what will be the next step for each student? What student data will the teacher need to collect while teaching the lesson in order to provide effective feedback? What independent work should be assigned to practice new learning?

There are essentially two parts to a learning objective—*a measurable skill and a concept or topic.* Examples of skills include a student's ability to interpret, describe, write, create, analyze, compare, or order. In other words, the verbs in the standard. Skills do *not* include the term "understand" as in "the student will understand fractions." Understanding is difficult to measure. After the skill, a concept is stated. Concepts include content such as fractions, major battles in the Civil War, or figurative language.

A measurable skill in the learning objective is important because once a teacher determines the skill and concept to be taught, she must determine what it will look like when a student has accomplished the objective. In other words, what will the skill look like where the student is practicing it successfully and what will the summative assessment look like? How does the teacher define "successfully?" Will success look different for different students?

The second part of creating the learning objective is the topic or big idea of the lesson. In other words, what the content is such as decimals, Civil War, metamorphosis, or figurative language. While the skill is always a verb, the concept is always a noun.

Sometimes standards contain more than one objective. For example:

Describe characters in a story (e.g., their traits, motivations, or feelings) and explain how their actions contribute to the sequence of events.

There are two objectives in this one standard: describe the characters and explain how characters' actions contribute to the sequence of events in the story.

Here's another example:

Use verbs to convey a sense of past, present, and future.

There are three learning objectives in this standard: use past, present, and future tense verbs.

Learning objectives must be differentiated from activity statements. For example, a teacher may provide instructions such as "complete page 3–4 in math text, read a story, or do a worksheet on multiplication." These are activities which may put standards into action, but the completion of these tasks are not learning objectives.

Once a learning objective has been determined with a measurable skill and concept or topic, the measurable skill then becomes the guiding focus for the lesson. Determining that skill will help establish the strategies for direct instruction, the choice of independent work, the checking for understanding questions, and the outline of the summative assessment. In other words, the measurable skill sets the students up for learning whatever the new content will be in a direct instruction lesson. If the content is not new and for practice instead, it is imperative that the teacher knows the difference.

When was the new content taught? Yesterday? Last week? If so, then the teacher should have some data from the CFUs and know if this is a reteaching or review lesson. The CFU data a teacher collects during a lesson informs instructional decision-making during the lesson and long afterwards.

A next step in designing the lesson is to plan for how the skill will be developed. Decisions a teacher makes at this point are determined by the type of knowledge inherent in the learning objective. When there are steps to a skill such as adding fractions, writing an essay, or calculating the circumference of a circle, this is called procedural knowledge. Declarative knowledge, on the other hand, is to provide information or facts. For example, describe the stages of metamorphosis, analyze the major events of the Civil War, or compare the characters in two stories.

Each type of knowledge informs how the teacher will teach the skill during the whole class lesson, especially what examples to use when modeling the skill.

Here is another sample learning objective:

Describe the four stages in the metamorphoses of butterflies.

The skill is to *describe*. The teacher must determine what that means in the context of the lesson. Does it mean define each stage in writing, by drawing a picture of each stage of the process, orally reciting the stages, or even possibly all three? If so, the teacher must provide examples of each form during the lesson—define on paper, draw, and speak. Even "define on paper" also has underlying decisions. Does this mean match the definition with the word on a worksheet? Or does he mean write a definition from scratch? What elements must be included in a drawing? As you can see, forethought into these parts of the lesson is crucial and improves student learning because it is much harder for the student to fall though alignment cracks.

Another decision in the lesson design is the choice of sample exercises. How many exercises should be done? Should a teacher include extras in case the skill is more difficult than the teacher determined, and students need more time? These are important decisions. Sometimes teachers have to "wing it," or come up with examples on the spot. But making these decisions in the planning stage makes the lesson much more efficient and effective. This front-loading gives the teacher an opportunity to check with the skill level on a Bloom's chart, ask his colleagues, or otherwise evaluate the skill/example alignment.

If the content includes steps in a process, such as mathematical or scientific equations, aligning the steps becomes just as important. Having an example that illustrates the skill, including a non-example, and having a CFU at the end of each step may seem laborious but it keeps students focused. It also enables the teacher to see where students falter and which step may be a stumbling block for students.

Remember. The skill level must be aligned to the independent work assigned to students. This may be independent work accomplished anytime a student does not have direct teacher input: during small group time, center time, or even homework. Using the data a teacher has collected during the lesson from CFUs should guide whether or not independent work is even assigned.

Often a teacher sends students off to do independent work while she works with small groups. Constant interruptions by the students doing independent work can greatly disrupt the time teachers have with small groups. In many instances, these students ask a lot of questions because they do not understand how to complete the independent work, especially if it looks different than what was taught in whole class instruction.

When these interruptions happen, a teacher should reflect on whether or not these interruptions are a classroom management issue or an academic issue. If it is an academic issue, the teacher may only need to clarify a small mistake, but if the student did not understand the concept or was not taught how to execute the verb of the skill, then basic confusion ensues. On top of the confusion, classroom management problems arise since most children will misbehave rather than admit they cannot do the work. At this point, teachers may need to monitor and adjust the lesson plan for that day.

The three parts of the lesson design—learning objective, practice, and assessment of the learning objective—must be aligned. This is especially true when the final assessment will be via a formal test such as a benchmark or end of course exam. If any part is out of alignment, students are set up for failure. They must be prepared to reveal their new knowledge a variety of ways which the teacher has to build into her design before the lesson, not as an afterthought.

Failure to follow this course of action is precisely why students form gaps in their learning. There is a plethora of websites on how to write learning objectives. This design skill is also taught in undergraduate school and it is included in all instructional manuals. Yet this skill is fundamentally lost in the classroom when not dissected to this minute level. Sometimes this design skill is implied, or vaguely understood, but precision of thought and action are needed so instructional decisions do not become hit and miss.

Does this take time to do right? Of course, it does. But as with any skill, with practice, collaboration, professional dialogue, and support, it becomes much more natural. The process of producing written learning objectives as an ongoing practice ensures beginning teachers, veteran teachers, and teachers new to the school, and all others are on the same path to improve student learning. Something so simple is a powerful tool for teachers which can produce enhanced learning for students.

So far, producing a written learning objective has only been described as an isolated activity. At this point, this skill needs to be put into the larger context of Bloom's Taxonomy, a classification system for the different objectives and skills that educators set for their students. There are six hierarchical levels of this taxonomy meaning that each level is dependent on reaching prerequisite skills at a lower level. Bloom levels are: Remember, Understand, Apply, Analyze, Evaluate, and Create. Each level contains verbs that help teachers structure a lesson. It is a powerful tool because it helps explain the process of learning.

For example, before you can understand a concept, you must remember it. To apply a concept you must understand it, to evaluate a process you must have analyzed it, and to create a valid conclusion, you must have completed a thorough evaluation. There are verb tables in every beginning teacher's textbooks that help identify which verb/skill align with what level in Bloom's. Not every lesson moves through the hierarchy of skills—that would become tedious quickly.

The instructional decisions teachers make about how to write and apply learning objectives within Bloom's context comes from the four key components a teacher uses to make these decisions—professional judgment of students' learning environments, knowledge of individual students' learning needs, data story of individual students, and research context.

A constraining structure in the school day is time, and all teachers want to have more time. Instructional time is at a premium when the structure of schools remains the same but teachers are constantly given more things to teach in the same amount of time. It is particularly disconcerting when there is an exact schedule of minutes per subject surrounding other happenings during the day like recess, lunch time, changing classes, or fire drills. This makes adjusting lessons such as reteaching skills and concepts that students missed during a whole class session difficult to do when a clock is running.

In the lesson design, the teacher has to consider how long it will take a student to learn a new skill and concept. This is not an easy task. It depends on what gaps a student may have that inhibit brain transfer (more on this aspect in the next chapter), what other activities are happening that day, and what transitions students will make from one activity to another.

Transition time is one way a teacher can actually add more instructional time to a lesson. There is a term heard often in schools that is taken with differing degrees of seriousness. That term is "bell to bell." What that means is maximizing instructional time from "bell to bell" but in practice making sure students are doing something the entire time allotted for a lesson. That "something" is where the teacher has most of the control. The something can be a series of discrete activities or it can be a well thought out lesson.

Examples of transitions can be moving from large to small groups, students going to retrieve digital devices from a cart in the classroom between lessons, or even lining up to go to lunch or change classes. For the most part, these transitions fall into a classroom management category where teachers have developed some type of procedure to ensure it goes smoothly.

"Smoothly" doesn't always happen so teachers are frequently invoking some behavior management program or sometimes yelling or even threatening students with negative consequences. But if a teacher does not get these transitions going smoothly, it interferes with instructional time. Another instructional time killer is when administrators permit lessons to be interrupted with loudspeaker announcements, allowing interruptions from outside the class delivering information or resources, or students leaving and entering classrooms.

While the teacher cannot control those actions, she can control the actions inside the classroom to improve use of instructional time. One way to control the actions is to put thought into the how and why he or she makes instructional decisions.

We are now brought full circle in our look at the educator's mirepoix of curriculum, instruction, and assessment. This chapter took a close look at instruction, dissecting it at a precise level so teachers can examine and improve their practice. The heart of instruction is design and delivery. Teachers have the absolute power to make it their own as instructional leaders.

PRACTICAL MATTERS

1. Unfortunately, writing explicit learning objectives in the development of lesson plans is one of those actions that gets lost quickly in the fast pace of daily teaching. It is also in danger of becoming mechanical rather than a strategic action when the teacher merely peruses the list of verbs and sticks them into a lesson plan or copies and pastes from a standards list or an outside-provided curriculum guide. Teachers can dig out their old textbooks from their undergraduate days, search online, or even ask colleagues to review and study examples of basic learning objectives.

Teacher should make a habit of bringing their learning objectives to planning meetings and have professional dialogue around determining the skills, what will it look like when a student masters a skill, how to align resources and assessment with the skill, what level of Bloom's is aligned with this objective, and how will the level be raised for students to gain a deeper understanding of the skill.

2. Take an in-depth look at Bloom's Taxonomy. This seems like a no brainer since every teacher is usually aware of this staple of education. But how many teachers still use it as a daily lesson design guide? How do teachers use it as a strategic practice rather than a mechanical one of merely choosing a verb from the chart and calling it a day? How does the taxonomy apply to everyday learning situations in which a teacher has multiple types of students in the classroom whose needs must be addressed? It gets complicated quickly, but the teaching profession is built on this fundamental concept of learning and teachers would be well served to revisit it regularly.

Bloom's Taxonomy is hierarchal, meaning that learning at the higher levels is dependent on having attained prerequisite knowledge and skills at lower levels. But it would be tedious to take students through each level for every lesson. It is important for teachers to know their students and make a determination as to which level a lesson needs to begin. At this point, teachers may notice that some verbs on a table may be associated with several levels of the taxonomy. As stated earlier in the chapter, it is the skill, action, or activity teachers will teach using that verb that determines the Bloom's Taxonomy level. What will the learning of that verb or level of Bloom's look like when the student is successful?

Something else to consider is that many times teachers ask questions during a lesson that are higher-level questions. But oftentimes teachers accept lower-level answers. By planning ahead of time how a teacher will respond in this situation, teachers can be ready with prompts, or rephrasing strategies that ensure students answer at the level at which the question was asked.

3. One of the words that have made it into education jargon these days is "rigor." Teachers know that it is needed in the classrooms because curriculum standards require it. Teachers hear often that workplaces and colleges also require it. But what does it mean? Having a professional conversation around this word alone is a useful activity. How each teacher defines this word can make a huge difference in lesson design if everyone has a different idea about what it looks like in the classroom. Oftentimes, teachers think that it means giving 100 mathematics problems rather than 50 or giving more homework if a student does not do well with the content in class. Some even think that it only belongs in higher-level classes such as calculus or Advance Placement courses.

The definition of "rigor" puts a sharp focus on instructional design because how a teacher views it creates the learning environment. Just as doing CFUs regularly and strategically during a lesson establishes that no student is *not* allowed to *not* know as discussed in chapter 3, a teacher's understanding of "rigor" establishes that *each* student in the class is expected to learn at high levels.

Many teachers say they have "high expectations" that students can learn at a high level. Operationalizing this term begins with understanding the term "rigor" by establishing that *every* student in a school has the potential to be his or her best. A natural place to begin for teachers to put this belief in practice is to use steps described in the CFU process. CFUs are a rigorous process that all students.

4. Teachers that are ready to take a deeper dive into identifying levels of rigor for assessment will want to investigate Webb's Depth of Knowledge (DoK) framework. Dr. Norman Webb developed the DoK in the late 90s to categorize activities according to the level of complexity in thinking. There are four levels of knowledge: Level 1—Acquired Knowledge, Level 2—Knowledge Application, Level 3—Analysis, and Level 4—Augmentation, usually represented on a wheel that represents the amount of thinking required for a given question or task. Aligning questions to different DoK levels facilitates higher-order thinking and deeper learning for students.

Using this framework, however, is a complex task and one that needs much discussion to understand and practice to implement well. As with all frameworks, they can be superficial if teachers are unwilling or unable to take on the deeper learning they themselves must do first before using effectively with students. Teachers must get beyond the verb chart for Bloom's Taxonomy and the wheel for DoK for either of these frameworks to be effective for student learning.

Administrators, as well as teachers, will also want to check out work by Dr. Karin Hess. As a curriculum and assessment expert, she has always been concerned that higher order verbs or thinking levels did not always result in learning tasks requiring deeper understanding or strategic thinking. From this concern, she developed the Hess Cognitive Rigor Matrix. This Matrix helps teachers apply what cognitive demand might look like in classrooms across several content areas. She has developed toolkits to introduce cognitive rigor and aide teachers in planning instruction and designing assessments.

5. *Teachers and administrators can create their own lesson planning template.* One that meets the needs of both teachers and administrators. It is a difficult process. A lesson plan format that integrates all of the steps outlined in this book could easily be between seven to eight pages. Although the goal is to have teachers learn the process by practicing the steps for several lessons, teachers may balk mightily.

Lesson plans need to be simple enough to follow but comprehensive enough to know if the lesson is thorough. It needs to be more than just a page in a textbook or the name of a worksheet but certainly less than 7–8 pages. If the lesson plan is a mechanical gesture that teachers "have to turn in" without a strategic focus, it becomes meaningless. When teachers are involved in the plan's design and administrators remind everyone of the strategic goal for lesson planning—which needs to be more than "something a substitute can follow"—it is more a professional resource for teachers instead of a burden.

When all in the school are following a similar format for how a lesson should flow, how checking for understanding is embedded, and how teachers are making instructional decisions, observers can go into any classroom, at any time, and determine "where" a teacher is in a lesson. Just by looking at student work, one observer should be able to determine the lesson objective for the day and the students' progress toward that objective because the student work matches the skill and content of that objective.

This is much more meaningful than if a teacher has merely written the objective on the board or if the teacher has put a copy of the lesson plan by the door. But most importantly, having a well written lesson plan that translates into effective student learning respects teachers as professionals, as the instructional leaders of the school.

6

How Is Effective Instruction Delivered?

Hollywood has created the myth of the super teacher. The teacher that stands in front of the class and is so engaging, so knowledgeable, so charismatic, that the student's attention is rapt and focused. In movies using real teachers as models, the movie characters are usually martyrs, inspiring students beyond what most of us can only dream of. Think *Dead Poets Society*, *Stand and Deliver*, or *Mr. Holland's Opus*. Although all teachers aspire to be like those star teachers to some degree, it is a tough standard to uphold.

On a more real and personal level, educators all have known, been taught by, taught with, and admired from afar a special teacher. When asked their favorite teacher, most people can name a specific teacher, recall his or her name, the grade taught, and the circumstances of the learning experiences in his or her classroom. For some it was a grade-school teacher, for others that teacher appeared in college or graduate school. Some educators have been fortunate enough to have been colleagues with a great teacher or two or three.

When most people are asked to remember who favorite teachers are and why they are chosen, responses include "he cared and it showed," "she made a difference in my life," "he believed in me," "she pushed me to do my best," "she created a safe place," "he brought out my creativity (or inner mathematician or scientist)," or "she went beyond teaching and made sure I had clothes or food."

Some favorite teachers challenged their students to go beyond what the students thought they were capable of doing. These teachers are often remembered with fondness in students' later years but seldom while the students are being "pushed" to excel. Whatever the reason, those teachers made an impression and are considered "gifted."

Memories of favorite teachers involve strong emotion: those favorite teachers made their students feel better about themselves. Often those special teachers came along at a time when their students needed another adult to care about them. These memories and strong emotions attached to them remind us that a positive emotional connection with a teacher is fundamental to the profession.

Often "good" teachers have some combination of emotionally connecting with their students and using effective pedagogy. While these "good" teachers often rely on instinct, there probably is a knowledge of how students learn that drives their practice. Relying on "gut" or "instinct" alone, though, is a haphazard and inefficient means of making sure all students receive effective instruction. Why not have all teachers practice effective pedagogical techniques consciously on a regular basis, as a collective practice?

This collective practice of effective strategies relies on using best evidence for any and all instructional decisions, fidelity to those practices, a less-is-more approach to professional development initiatives, and ongoing training of teachers in effective, evidence-based strategies like wait time. Focusing on whole faculty needs, rather than individuals, followed by faculty reinforcement sessions, can enable schools to see large gains in student learning, teacher morale, and overall teacher effectiveness.

All of those gains do not happen in a vacuum: they happen when deliberate, mindful decisions are made by teachers, and by their administrators, to wholeheartedly move in that direction. Administrators need to support teachers trying to make changes in their daily practice by providing time and opportunities to practice, monitor, coach, and provide each other feedback on a continuous basis. When these actions become routine, they get woven into the culture of a school. When new teachers or administrators come on board, they are initiated into the culture for sustainability.

This collective practice of effective strategies happens when teachers and administrators are not tied to programs, new initiatives, or personalities but ensure that any new programs or initiatives that are brought into the school align with this collective practice. It is the foundation on which programs, resources, and other innovations are built on. This collective practice can restore and retain the teacher's role as the instructional leader, enabling him or her to make confident instructional decisions.

This from-the-inside school culture turns the current system on its head. Having teachers make the decisions about what new programs or initiatives to add to their curriculum is a game changer: by not jumping on bandwagons but amplifying a steady, coherent message that new programs and initiatives will be chosen by the teachers based on best evidence.

What does this collective practice look like in a classroom? Fidelity to effective practices begin with how teachers make instructional decisions. Instructional decisions made before, during, and after lesson delivery are crucial to whether or not students learn. All of a teacher's pedagogical knowledge comes into play in these moments of lesson delivery. They are collecting data using intentional questions as a checking for understanding, providing effective feedback, and making moment-to-moment decisions about pacing, differentiating, and which student needs extra help.

Teachers also are making decisions about who is ready for independent work and ready to practice without supervision. They are grouping students, regrouping those same students, and choosing appropriate materials for each group. These decisions happen daily and often "on the fly," based on when new information is received. It is no wonder teachers are tired at the end of a teaching day! In the remainder of this chapter, we will dig down into how delivery is structured as a teacher makes preparations and then delivers a new lesson.

In the previous chapter, it was emphasized that there are important elements that go into "front loading" a lesson, or into the instructional design. Once those decisions are made, teachers are ready to plan the delivery, or teaching, of that lesson. A reminder: the delivery strategies in this chapter work best for a direct, whole class lesson when new content is being taught.

Direct, whole group instruction is foundational in all models of teaching—project-based learning, inquiry based, collaborative learning, regardless what the new learning method du jour may be. Whatever the program model, students need to learn content such as how to multiply two-digit numbers, how to analyze text, or understand the scientific method. The second reminder is that the strategies given in this chapter do not happen "on the fly" during the lesson, they too are front loaded and thought out during the lesson design, then delivered during the lesson itself.

This does not mean that a teacher may not monitor and adjust the lesson. It means that there must be a foundation of strategies for delivery that is built into every lesson and practiced with fidelity. As teachers gain confidence, and see results, he or she will be able to make those adjustments in the lesson delivery.

Evidence-based delivery strategies have a positive effect on student learning. These strategies are practiced in a hierarchal order, using what is known about how the brain learns. When steps are skipped or badly executed, gaps form in a child's learning process. Note that checking for understanding questions are included in each step to assure continuity. Teachers will need to collect CFU data at each step to assure students are in the same place in the process. Teachers will also need this data to inform their pacing and possible adjustments to the lesson delivery.

Following are the steps for the foundation of lesson delivery:

1. One of the most powerful strategies to practice at the beginning of any lesson is to teach the learning objective. This is not teaching the lesson—that follows this step—but requiring that students understand what they will learn

in the lesson and how they will learn it. It is a primary reason to have the learning objective written on the board. The students have not been taught the content yet so they are not required to repeat the content of the lesson in a checking for understanding but repeat/read/paraphrase/state the skill and topic of the learning objective.

This is especially powerful when the teacher can guarantee that the child will leave the classroom knowing the why and how of a lesson before they are required to practice the new skill and content independently in class or for homework. Imagine children actually doing their independent work because they practiced with the teacher, she did a checking for understanding and made sure no one was assigned independent work unless she was sure they could do it successfully on their own.

To teach the learning objective the teacher does a check for understanding by asking the question "what are we going to learn today" *after she or he has stated the learning objective*. If the learning objective is written on the board, the teacher may simply read it before asking students the objective in a random sampling and tell students to use it as a prompt if needed. Be sure not to ask "what are we going to *do*" because that implies the activity they will be doing such as completing a workbook page or reading from a textbook.

"What we are going to learn today" states that students are going to learn new content, add it to our short- and long-term memory, and practice the new learning with the teacher today before they leave the classroom. When students know what they are going to learn from a direct teaching lesson, they can prepare their brain, their attitude, and their bodies to work on learning, confident the teacher will not let them down.

It also clarifies the lesson, reducing vagueness. It is a joyful occurrence to walk into a classroom, or ask a student in the hallway, or at home in the evening, "what did you learn today?" and have students give a specific answer. An answer such as "I learned how to multiply two-digit numbers," or "I learned the stages of metamorphosis in caterpillars." Parents can attest that the answer is usually a blank stare or some hodgepodge of activities rather than the content of a lesson or lessons. The uninterested looks from students happens more and more as they advance in school and outgrow the enthusiasm of a six-year-old excited to learn how to read or do simple math.

Often teachers think it may take too long, or if done for every lesson, becomes robotic for students. This is a time for the art of teaching to mix with the science of teaching. How can a teacher make this necessary learning task appeal to students? How can the teacher emphasize why it works, how their brains work, and how it helps them be more metacognitive about how they learn? Teaching students these skills about how they learn in conjunction with the subject area content is a powerful combination.

2. The next step of the lesson should be to help children connect past learning to new learning. New learning must be built on students' experiences, interests, and background knowledge before a lesson is taught. It provides a context and connection for students. Teachers need to "prime" students' brains for the new learning. All new learning builds on prior learning. Making this connection between what a student already knows and the new content they are going to learn is called activation of prior knowledge.

Activating prior knowledge is a brain-based step that facilitates the retrieval of pertinent information from students' long-term memories that will make it easier for them to learn new content. Once this information is retrieved, it is put into working memory, so students are thinking about it intentionally. If a teacher does not provide the stimulus to activate this prior knowledge, student will have difficulty learning the new content. Hence, another opportunity for learning gaps to form.

Teachers must also be careful not to ask students what they know about the new content before it is taught. For example, if the learning objective is to "describe the process of photosynthesis," a teacher would not activate prior knowledge by asking students what they know about photosynthesis. This is the new content. Instead, for younger students, a teacher may show a picture of a plant and ask students what a plant needs to grow such as air and water. For older students, it may be activating previously learned content such as the meaning of chloroplasts and carbon dioxide.

In the design phase, a teacher must determine what prerequisite skills are needed to teach the new content. For example, if the new content is the Pythagorean theory, then prerequisite skills may include defining hypotenuse and knowing the difference between a right angle and other types of angles. These prerequisite skills must be brought to the forefront of their brains before they learn the new content.

But what if students do not have the prerequisite skills? Perhaps they did not learn them in prior grades when they were grade level curriculum standards. If that is the case, the teacher must do a quick lesson with checking for understanding before proceeding with new content. If the teacher does not do these quick lessons, then the student will not be able to retain the new information because there is nothing in the brain to "hook" on. When teaching learning-challenged students, this becomes a primary concern.

If too much time is taken teaching grade-level knowledge that is from a lower grade, teachers worry that no time will be left teaching current grade-level content on which standardized testing is based. It is a catch-22 because if students' gaps are not filled prior to the new learning they will not be able to work at grade level. Spending time on determining prerequisite skills in the design phase is a necessary element.

Once a teacher can determine these prerequisite skills prior to the delivery of new content, he or she can probably know which students will need extra tutoring. He or she can assign these prerequisite skill-learning objectives with a resource teacher, an assistant in the classroom, a student teacher, or perhaps to an after-school tutor or program to work on before the new lesson. Having purposeful work that connects the missing prerequisite skills with new lessons will benefit the student greatly if it can be accomplished outside the classroom, providing the teacher more time to teach on grade level.

A distinction must be made between activating prior knowledge and motivating a student to learn new content. Activating prior knowledge is the practice of connecting what students already know to new learning. This is a connection made in the brain and is an intentional element in the design but always in the beginning of a new lesson delivery. It is usually woven into the introduction of a lesson.

Other parts of the introduction may be showing a video, asking their opinion on the topic or providing some background to the topic. These strategies are meant to get the students interested in the topic or content, to motivate them to want to pay attention. It is important that the teacher be able to make this distinction so each can be delineated as such in the planning phase.

In the introduction to a lesson, teachers oftentimes need to pre-teach vocabulary. At this point in the lesson, unless it is a specific learning objective that has students defining a word, teachers are only pronouncing the word for the students, defining the word, and giving examples. Reading vocabulary words in context is a primary literacy strategy. However, it helps students when they confront a new word if they have had the teacher pronounce the word aloud and give some background as well as context of the topic. Reviewing vocabulary after the lesson or as an extension of the lesson with vocabulary squares or word webs, for example, can reinforce vocabulary that students now can use in context rather than trying to have students know the definitions before the lesson.

In addition to making connections in the brain between new learning and academic knowledge, activating prior knowledge can also be practiced using students' experiences in knowledge from everyday life. For example, in a kindergarten class, the teacher is teaching students to identify the color "red." She or he may hold up an apple, a strawberry, or other red fruit that students have eaten. Students then make a connection between a red object and the word "red."

This is key to using this strategy—it must be an experience all students have had to be equitable and to make connections in the brain. If teachers were using the prior experience of flying on a plane to connect with a science lesson on Bernoulli's Principle, she or he would have to know ahead of time that almost all of the students had been on a plane. If not, the activating prior knowledge with an experience "falls flat."

The introduction to a lesson and activating prior knowledge should not take more than eight to ten minutes since most of the lesson needs to be focused on the new content. But skipping this part can create learning gaps and cause confusion later on after the teacher has moved on to other parts of the lesson. A teacher must make this step a "must do" for every lesson teaching new content.

3. Now it's time to get into the heart of the lesson—new content. How a teacher delivers this component depends upon the nature of the new content. Knowledge can be roughly divided into two types: procedural knowledge that requires steps on how to do something, such as multiplying or writing, or declarative knowledge that is informational or a set of facts. The skill in the learning objective will inform the teacher what type of knowledge is inherent in the new content. Most importantly, it informs the teacher what tasks he or she will perform during the delivery of the lesson.

If the content includes procedural knowledge, the teacher teaches the steps of a process such as adding, or multiplying, or writing a sentence. If the content includes declarative knowledge, the teacher provides an explanation, states a set of facts, or a resource that accomplishes that part of the lesson. Declarative knowledge usually requires that the teacher provide a tool to organize this information such as a graphic organizer.

Whatever the knowledge type, the most powerful strategy a teacher delivers during this phase of the lesson is *modeling*, showing students how the skill is used in the context of the new learning. It is not enough to talk about it, a teacher must show how it is done along with checking for understanding all along the process. A teacher can use examples, and often when teaching procedural knowledge, many examples are needed.

It is imperative that the teacher show how the learning objective is accomplished, in other words, model the skill level stated in the learning objective. Using modeling and CFUs at each step before students work independently will provide an exemplar for students because the teacher has shown what it looks like when the learning objective is being executed successfully.

The modeling must use the same resource students will be using in their independent practice. To model with one resource while asking students to use another independently is the equivalence of a bait and switch and not only creates or expands on learning gaps but also creates ill will and negative attitudes toward learning, the teacher, or both.

For example, suppose that for the lesson to describe the stages of metamorphosis the teacher decided that students should be able to orally describe each stage. During the lesson, he or she can show drawings of each stage, describe them aloud, and check for understanding that the students can orally describe. If, on the assessment however, students are required to draw each stage and label it, then that is a bait and switch. It may have been assigned as homework perhaps, but if not intentionally taught by the teacher, it becomes a hit or miss for students.

In fact, having a fundamental understanding of how memory is retained and how to apply it in the classroom is a necessary skill every teacher should have in her repertoire. *Memory systems include sensory memory, which only lasts a few seconds, working memory that lasts only about 30 seconds unless rehearsed or processed, and long-term memory which has an unlimited capacity.* The key with memory retention is the transfer from one system to another ending in long-term memory. A teacher that understands this concept uses several strategies to accomplish these transfers—repetition, mnemonics, rehearsal, and audio and visual stimuli, usually called cognitive strategies.

Cognitive strategies are integrated throughout a lesson to enable the brain to remember new knowledge. Many teachers use these randomly, but more intentional, consistent use of these strategies is key to helping students retain information. Examples of cognitive strategies include mnemonic devices, use of colors to delineate words or steps, creating anchor charts that will be used as a reference for independent work, or using a graphic organizer to organize large amounts of information such as details on a Civil War battle in a social studies lesson, or to analyze information such as main idea and supporting details in a written text.

More sophisticated cognitive strategies include concept maps and mind maps. Other strategies a teacher can use to help students remember new content is to have students draw pictures, create visual models such as flowcharts, or keep a journal for each subject where a student keeps their notes, drawings, and visual aids in one place. Science notebooking is a good example.

Other examples of cognitive strategies are using associations such as metaphors, using clues in reading comprehension, or even underlining key words or concepts in a reading can help put new learning into short-term memory. Cognitive strategies do not have to be elaborate, but they do need to be designed into the lesson intentionally.

4. Once a teacher has modeled the skill stated in the learning objective with the new content, it is time to give students an opportunity to practice the skill with the new knowledge while the teacher is monitoring. This fourth step is called *guided practice* and has been a staple of lessons for decades. However, without intention and checking for understanding questions, it can be too short and oftentimes left out entirely.

Guided practice means the teacher is directing the whole class to perform the lesson's skill before the student works independently. Students are working on the same problem at the same time and she has a CFU for each step or new information. The teacher can determine if more repetitions or examples are needed and by whom so she can slowly release students for independent work.

Oftentimes, this step is left out and students move from the whole class lesson to independent work. Teachers then usually proceed to answer students' questions or work with students independently: a highly inefficient practice. Trying to address each students' individual problems can be chaotic when many students need help at the same time. Guided practice can eliminate this chaos.

5. The fifth and final step in the lesson is *closure*. This is an important step because the teacher will be making decisions about who is ready to do independent work successfully. The checking for understanding data that a teacher has been collecting throughout the lesson may reveal that some students are not ready. If that is the case, then those students will either need to be retaught in a small group before doing the independent work or not given the assignment as homework.

This is a different approach than usually seen in the classroom. Oftentimes, all students are assigned the same independent work, even knowing that some students will have difficulty. These students will be less likely to return the work when it is due. Who wants to spend time in frustration? Why would teachers ask students to do schoolwork that they cannot do successfully on their own? Differentiating assignments is more work for teachers but necessary.

Another ineffective method often observed for closure is the teacher giving a summary of the day's lesson. But closure should be about the students letting *the teacher* know they know how to do the work successfully. Maybe it is one more problem on a whiteboard. Maybe it is one more random check with more nonvolunteers. One thing it is not is what is called an exit slip. Sometimes an exit slip is assigned as a final checking for understanding but its fatal flaw is that it is usually handed to the teacher on the way out the door.

At that point, the teacher cannot make corrections, cannot reteach, cannot provide effective feedback. And the frustration will set in for the student when they try to practice the new content. Perhaps a better use of the exit slip would be a reflection for the student on his or her metacognitive processes used that day to learn the new content.

The last part of closure is assigning student independent work. Seen most often in observations is the teacher explaining new content, maybe modeling, then sending the students directly to independent work with the intention of helping individual students as they work. When more than a couple of students either did not understand how to do the independent work or needed directions clarified, it quickly became difficult to manage the situation.

Even when students are raising their hands waiting for the teacher to come around to help them, they are losing time to work and if they wait too long, can get bored and move on to being fidgety that can lead to misbehavior. Oftentimes the teacher finds herself reteaching the same lesson to individual students many times over which is time consuming and ineffective.

This can all be avoided with a carefully planned guided practice session where the teacher is gathering data to determine who is ready for independent work and who needs to be pulled aside for a small group reteaching. When students know how to do the work, then they will spend less time procrastinating, waving their hands, or other methods to get the teacher's attention.

Another positive outcome of the thoughtful planning of guided practice is that when the independent work is assigned as homework, more students will be able to do it correctly at home or away from class. Oftentimes students do not complete homework because they do not know how to do the work. It may have been too long since they worked on it in class, and the older they get, the more likely they will not attempt it at all.

The next day, the teacher then spends instructional time "going over homework" but actually reteaching the content because it was not learned during the previous lesson. This sets up another round of catch up where students fall through the cracks, learning gaps form, and the teacher moves on due to pressure to "get it all in" before testing.

This component of the lesson will take up the most time and is the most fluid because the teacher is constantly monitoring who is keeping up and who is not. Small groups can be different from last lesson. If random checking for understanding questions reveal that more than a few students are not "getting it," or perhaps "got it" faster than the teacher had predicted, instructional time could change and the teacher must monitor and adjust.

Just as important as providing cognitive strategies during the lesson to help students remember, is spreading out practice in such a way that they retain the information beyond the test and can use it to build new knowledge upon down the road. Learning is not remembering new content for a test and promptly forgetting it, but being able to build new neural pathways in the brain for the long stretch. When that new learning is meaningful, relatable, and makes sense to the student, there is a much better chance those pathways are formed. This can give new meaning and structure to how and what teachers assign for bell work, homework, or differentiation work.

PRACTICAL MATTERS

1. Making a plan for "front loading" a lesson to include these teaching strategies in this order will require deliberate intentions to the planning process via the lesson plan format. However, if each step was outlined completely, the lesson plan format would be long and tedious. But doing this on a regular basis, with say, every third lesson or once a week, can instill the thinking process in the teacher's mind and thus create a new mindset and thinking pattern.

Administrators should be transparent about why lesson plans should be "turned in" and how, when, and why feedback will be provided. This established trust between the teachers and administrators and goes a long way in establishing the type of culture that encourages and nurtures these types of professional conversations.

Creating a teacher resource of cognitive strategies for every standard and learning objective is a project the entire faculty can work on. This cognitive strategy resource can be added to as new strategies are tried in the classrooms and provide enough selection so teachers and students do not get bored. Being specific about cognitive strategies and how they enable students to remember new content enables teachers to integrate into a lesson with intent.

2. Creating and teaching mini lessons with students on how their brain works can help students discover how they learn, which cognitive strategies work best for them, and how they can be accountable for their own learning in meaningful ways. Students can keep a journal where they can record and analyze which strategies and techniques work best for them. Not feelings about their learning—although they are important too—but thinking about how their brain worked during the lesson. This also fits well with social and emotional intelligence emphasis happening in education.

3. There is an opportunity to help children master prerequisite skills prior to new content taught in the classroom by making effective use of students' time outside of the classroom. Teachers can prepare work and resources aligned with prerequisite skills for others who work with those children in resource, after school, tutoring, or any other time children will be with another teacher. These can also be opportunities for students to practice newly learned skills under the supervision of a trained instructor. Connections between and among the primary teacher and all other resources the child comes in contact with are important to establish so information goes across the school and community.

7

Where Does Technology Fit?

Have you entered a building or a mall and had to walk through two sets of doors? These two sets of doors are called an arctic entry and were first used by natives in cold areas of the world, such as Alaska, when it was discovered that the cold air would get trapped in that space and not blow into the main living area. This discovery stays with us today, even in warmer climates, albeit with a modern twist as a way to save electricity. The modern equivalent in housing is sometimes called a mudroom, or a small room in the entryway to shed coats and shoes before entering the main part of the house, that traps the cold air from the warmth of the house.

Humans have been inventing things since the beginning of time when they made tools from stone, wood, antlers, and bones ten million years ago. All of these inventions have made life better and more efficient. These inventions have included not just mudrooms but also machines and defined many of our historical ages such as the Stone Age and the Industrial Age.

All of these inventions have a generic term: technology. The true definition of technology is "applying scientific knowledge for practical reasons." Fast forward to the 21st century when the term technology has become mainly associated with another meaning: electronic devices used as communication tools and a medium for delivering content such as radio programs and television shows.

The content delivered by these devices, such as news or games, as well as the ever-improving hardware itself, has been shaping the way humans think. Certainly, this has had an effect on society in general and education systems in particular. Thinking about this effect also puts what happens in classrooms into a much larger context, one that must take into account how technology has changed human brains and how that impacts learning.

In the late 1990s, billions of dollars were invested in computers by corporations to increase productivity. Robert Solow, a Nobel Prize winner for economics, studied this corporate investment and found that, in spite of the money invested, automation of existing business practices did not produce substantial increases in productivity. This phenomenon became known as the productivity paradox.

Businesses soon began to create new models and processes and productivity began to increase. There were entirely new ways of delivering services that leveraged what technology could do, and in turn, spurred new ways of thinking about how to do business. We experience the results of this today when we bank, shop, receive our news, communicate, even meet potential mates.

This has also been happening in education but to a much lesser degree. Occasionally a school district in the past couple of decades would embrace technology and add interactive whiteboards in classrooms or add computer labs in schools but for the most part, because adding technology devices was cost prohibitive, schools mostly stay on the sidelines as society leaps ahead with cell phones, laptop computers, and other devices.

Students are living in a society filled with technology but usually have to surrender those devices once they are in school. This has been happening since early 2000s. Then, and now, they spend their entire lives surrounded by and using video games, digital music players, video cameras, cell phones, and all the toys and tools of the digital age. The time they spend reading has decreased and the time spent playing video games and texting has increased. They have different expectations about the availability of people and data thanks to the vast amount of material on the internet and the ubiquity of email, text messaging, and cell phones.

The point is not that technology is good or bad, but that it is changing how humans think and learn. Educators need to see those changes clearly in order to take control of the profession and improve learning for students. Teachers may not like the changes but ignoring them is perilous to their careers.

To begin, it is important to understand how technology has changed human brains. In Nicholas Carr's 2010 book, *The Shallows: What the Internet Is Doing to Our Brains*, he explains it on a fundamental level. "A world defined by oral traditions is more social, unstructured, and multisensory; a world defined by written word is more individualistic, disciplined, and hyper visual. A world defined by testing, scrolling, and social feedback is addicted to stimulus, constantly forming and affirming expressions of identity, accustomed to waves of information."

From research in biology, it is known that the brain is being constantly reorganized based on the inputs it receives. This reorganization is called *neuroplasticity*. Indeed, there is evidence that television watching as well as other digital experiences at an early age by the vast majority of students physiologically changes the neuroplasticity in the brain, causing it to seek out more stimulating methods.

Since the 1950s when the first educational television was created, children have been entertained by television shows at home, such as Mr. Rogers, while going to school to be educated. When these two ideas merged, the term *edutainment* was coined. As much as all can agree that television is a fabulous educational tool, many teachers have feared they must become *Sesame Street* characters in their classrooms in order to get and keep their students' attention.

Marc Prensky, in 2001, coined the terms *digital natives* and *digital immigrants. The natives were the students, the "speakers" of the digital language of computers, video games, and the Internet. The teachers were the immigrants, adapting to the new environment that is different from their youth but maintain an "accent" such as turning to the Internet for information second rather than first or printing out emails or documents to edit rather than doing it on the screen.*

This characterization continues to this day, with many teachers still longing for the days before the Internet. This unwillingness to grasp how the student's perspectives and brains have changed and therefore change how they teach has been a struggle for a couple of decades now. While there are some teachers willing to change their perspective to accommodate these technology changes, there still is a long way to go to make it universal within the education community.

Schools, as well as businesses, need to adapt in times of significant change. While business and schools do not provide the same types of services, the business example of the productivity paradox mentioned previously informs the process of change for education, particularly when it comes to innovations in technology such as devices and their use in learning. Indeed, the painfully slow adaptation and implementation of technology in K–12 classrooms reached a critical point in the spring of 2020 when schools across the nation had to close down due to the coronavirus pandemic.

The lack of internet access, up-to-date devices, and teachers' knowledge or lack of knowledge about distance learning had a bright spotlight when schools were compelled to teach virtually. Many schools did not have the technology devices to send to students' homes, but most egregiously, many teachers did not have the skill set to switch their teaching from face-to-face to virtual. The skill set needed for virtual teaching, primarily technological literacy, is different than that of face-to-face teaching and has been largely ignored by teachers and administrators.

In the 1980s, computers were beginning to appear in schools and started gaining acceptance. These computers were placed in computer labs which meant the students were often physically separated from their teachers. "Computer time" was labeled a "related art" and consisted mainly of drilling and practice programs. Teachers developed a mindset that "computers" were a separate content area where students learned keyboarding skills rather than a learning tool.

This mindset was difficult to change even as computers slowly moved from the computer lab to a few in the back of the classroom. Fast forward to present day and many schools have moved to a one device per student model. Similar to trying to get students to "unlearn" misconceptions in order to teach new material, educators have had to "unlearn" that technology is more than devices or keyboarding or even interactive whiteboards.

Embracing technology as a powerful learning tool requires teachers to learn new skill sets and employ new practices. Rather than simply extending past practices, teachers must learn new organizational ways of working, challenging previously held values, and gaining new knowledge and skills. This type of change cannot be accomplished with another program, initiative, strategic plan, or new product. It begins with individual teachers and like-minded individual administrators that come together with a shared vision of infusing technology into instruction.

Making the shift from technical to adaptive change is difficult because we have become what Seymour Papert calls "techno centric." In other words, our instruction has become more focused on the technologies being used than on the students who are trying to use them. This dichotomy came about because using technology in schools was already a major shift.

Purchasing computers and other devices has also been expensive. Computers were purchased for labs only in the beginning as a cost-saving measure and an economy of scale. One lab could accommodate all students in a school if a rotating schedule was established. Doing so, however, caused educators to be conditioned to think computers are separate from the classroom. This was reinforced when students used computer education programs independently rather than in collaboration with a teacher. Thus, teachers developed the mindset that computers were learning machines to assist students apart from the classroom.

As devices became less costly, computer labs were dismantled and spread across campuses so that each classroom could have three or four. These were used on a rotating basis by students, still independent of lesson design or delivery integration. These computers in the back of the room were to provide "extra" practice for students or as a "reward" for completing work early.

Fast forward to today when a device for every student is not only feasible but slowly taking hold in many school districts. In districts implementing these 1:1 models (one device, one student) however, teachers are still having a difficult time seeing technology as a powerful tool that is integrated based on the learning goal. There exists still a techno-centric mindset in schools. This is exemplified by the ongoing practice of having district technology departments rather than instruction departments make most of the decisions about what technology devices and software to purchase.

Compounding this problem of changing teacher mindsets on using technology are the numerous educational software programs purchased by districts. These programs are added onto each year and requires teachers to figure out how to use a specific product rather than focusing on what technologies are needed for different types of learning. Remember that less is more. Teachers need the time and opportunity for in-depth professional development on only one or two initiatives to ensure lasting improvement in student learning.

Two important tools have come along in the last decade to aide teachers in integrating technology into instruction. The first, the SAMR model, was developed in the late 1980s and intended to provide teachers a way to self-reflect and refine their practices and pedagogy using instructional technology. This model was developed in 2010 by education researcher Ruben Puentedura. It lays out four tiers of online learning, presented roughly in order of their sophistication and transformative power: substitution, augmentation, modification, and redefinition.

When switching to an online format, teachers often focus on the first two levels, which involve replacing traditional materials with digital ones: converting lessons and worksheets into PDFs and posting them online, or recording lectures on video and making them available for asynchronous learning, for example. The last two levels of the SAMR model—modification and redefinition—are when students in classes find more novel and immersive uses for technology. They are creators and publishers of their own work across multiple forms of media, for example, or they are inviting professionals to provide feedback on their work products, or participating in digital forums with other peers around the world.

Although the SAMR model is an effective planning tool for teachers to use when designing lessons, they must not fall into the trap of thinking technology must be used in every lesson. They must use their professional judgment to decide the appropriate use of the technology. Sometimes an analog method will work as well or better than a digital method.

For example, a gallery walk with student work on chart paper hung around a room may be a better choice of collaboration than using a shared Google Doc. The SAMR model can be a guide for integrating technology but the teacher still must make instructional decisions based on her knowledge about the teaching environment. The key question a teacher must ask is if the technology use will enhance the learning process. If so, then it is appropriate to use.

The second tool, the TPACK framework, was introduced in 2006. This framework identifies three types of knowledge instructors need to combine for successful technology integration—technological, pedagogical, and content knowledge. This model, developed by educational researchers Mishra and Kohler, is designed around the idea that content (what you teach) and pedagogy (how you teach) must be the basis for any technology that you plan to use in your classroom to enhance learning.

Although it is often compared to the SAMR model, they are different in scope. Although the SAMR model is not intended to be linear, it is often perceived as such by teachers. The TPAK model shows us that there's a relationship between technology, content, and pedagogy, and the purposeful blending of them is key.

If districts are purchasing more technology and technology-dependent programs and there are excellent tools to help teachers with technology integration, why is that integration so slow to take root? Making adaptive change towards using technology as a powerful resource in teaching and learning is a large and ongoing goal of educators. Since the goal of this book is to restore and retain the teacher's role as instructional leader, it must be reiterated that reaching this goal requires a willing and open mind. Checking our assumptions and beliefs is the first step on the path for new ways of thinking and schooling.

In todays' times, internet use and device use are so ubiquitous, especially by youth, teachers either need to get comfortable with technology or find another career because "this too shall pass" will not work anymore. That sounds rather harsh, but a sentiment that is becoming a reality more and more in education. Many teachers left the profession in the aftermath of the pandemic in 2021 to the mandated use of technology to teach.

There are also some myths that have arisen from the increasing use of technology for teaching and learning. One is that putting devices into classrooms will magically transform weak teachers into effective teachers. This myth is promulgated when technology programs and devices are purchased by a district as a way to either prop up weak teachers or make some curricula "teacher proof," meaning an alternative to a weak teacher. If a teacher does not already understand and practice effective instructional design and delivery, there are no technology-based programs or devices that will magically change a weak teacher into a better one.

Many districts and schools that have implemented 1:1 policies failed to allow teachers to become proficient at effective instructional design before implementing this technology model. As a result, many classrooms became "tech centric," with teachers unable to make the transformation from a didactic method of teaching to using technology to teach.

Another myth is that technology is a silver bullet. Some want to believe that using technology in the classroom can fill all the learning gaps, solve childhood poverty, drastically improve test scores, or a myriad of other societal problems that schools are supposed to "fix" or ameliorate. Shifting our thinking from technology as a silver bullet to thinking about it as a powerful tool and resource to support teaching and learning can begin to dispel the myth. Yes, it is an expensive tool, an ever-changing tool, and difficult to understand at many levels about how it works and how it evolves. Yet in the end, it is a tool, just as paper, ink, typesetters, and other inventions changed how people taught and learned over the ages.

Teachers have many fears about using technology with students that need to be confronted, examined, and either validated or dismissed. The two major fears are (1) the technology will replace teachers, and (2) students know more about technology than they do so teachers cannot show that they are not the "expert" in their own classroom. Oftentimes both are present in the teacher's reluctance to use technology. In the early days of technology, teachers were given a "bye" if they resisted using technology. This can no longer be the case since technology is so ubiquitous on society and the education system.

A barrier to teachers renewing and retaining their role as instructional leader are these deep-felt fears about using technology in their classrooms. Many of these fears are not spoken out loud but manifested in their reluctance and in some cases, refusal to use technology for learning unless "forced." The root of some of these fears include:

1. Fear that technology will replace the teacher. This fear has been fueled by computer programs developed early in the use of computers in schools that were meant for students to use without a teacher, using algorithms to "teach" students. This is also reflected in broadly disseminated videos from groups such Kahn Academy that students can use to allegedly teach themselves.

Artificial intelligence has advanced greatly in the past decade so that robots can do many jobs that humans do such as working on an assembly line. In fact, Japan has produced a robot teacher that can take roll and say about 700 words. She can display about six emotions but she does not feel emotions. However, teaching requires understanding and caring that is not available in a robot. Robots are not inspirational—only a teacher can be in that role because he or she feels the emotions and cares for his or her students.

The fear that teachers can be replaced must be dispelled along with the misconception that the brain is like a computer. Throughout history the brain has been compared with different inventions such as telephone switchboards and water clocks. Now, in the modern age, the brain is being compared to computers.

Although there are some similarities, such as both have a memory to grow, there are also major differences. Computer memory grows by adding computer chips. Memories in the brain grow by stronger synaptic connections. Another example is that both can do math and other logical tasks. The computer is faster at doing logical things and computations. However, the brain is better at interpreting the outside world and coming up with new ideas and the brain is capable of imagination. Unlike computers, the brain does not passively respond to input and process data. It is a part of the body that does not represent information but constructs it.

2. *Fear that students know more about technology than teachers.* This scares teachers who need to be in control and see themselves as out of control if students are interacting with technology in ways the teachers may not understand. When schools started putting smaller devices in classrooms such as laptops and iPads, teachers demanded a dashboard so they could see where on the Internet students were at all times. These were developed for them by the market and purchased by districts, in particular ones that were adopting a 1:1 situation.

Are some students surfing shopping sites instead of researching a paper? Of course, they are. Are they distracted with all the choices they have when navigating the web? Of course, they are. But teachers can deal with these typical behaviors and treat them as classroom management decisions rather than instructional ones.

It is hard to wrap minds around the fact that society has gone from using a set of encyclopedias as the primary source of knowledge to having access to every resource in the world in a hand-held device. It is overwhelming. Being able to access information from literally anywhere in the world can be either a positive or negative experience, depending on your mindset. Students need research, filtering, and media literacy to wade through digital resources. It's a mind-boggling task to take on the teaching of these skills in a technology context but it is one teachers must boldly do.

Students today are familiar with technology from birth and have an innate sense of how to use technology for entertainment. But they have little to no experience on how to use technology to learn. Teachers must embrace and exploit the new ways students are engaged by teaching them to be metacognitive about how they learn with technology. But first teachers must know for themselves how they learn with technology.

For example, when teachers experience online learning, they learn what is boring, what is engaging, what skills the instructor needs to teach online that are different than face-to-face, how resources are used online and which ones transition from face-to-face instruction and which ones do not. This is not unlike the creation of *Sesame Street* when students started watching television to learn and their brains changed. Teachers can either lament and complain about the technology or figure out how to use it to benefit students the most.

It is easy to blame the "technology" when learning does not happen or argue that it complicates the profession. It can be frustrating when the structures and systems in place for using technology make it difficult for teachers to integrate technology such as when a school or institution has purchased a learning management system that is clunky and difficult to use.

Frustrations also come from trying to force fit old mindsets about teaching and learning into online instruction. The classic form of this is making a video of a lecture and putting it online. Oftentimes these system structures that impede efficient use and integration of technology are out of control of the teacher. Teachers need to know what works best for the teaching and learning environment in their classrooms and use that knowledge to inform decision makers about what technology to purchase. Articulating how he or she will integrate technology into her classroom and using research-based evidence to inform technology purchases and usage in the classroom will greatly improve the teacher's role as instructional leader.

Integrating technology is not only about putting devices in students' hands as learning tools. It involves an evolution in thinking about how technology can truly transform our traditional mindset about schools. For example, personalized learning is one of the newest terms applied in education today. It stems from the growing amount of technology use in classrooms and implies that classrooms are moving from teacher-centered to student-centered. It is difficult to observe this happening on a grand scale, however.

Most classrooms are still teacher-centered, even those with an abundance of technology tools. The promise of technology tools to transform learning recalls something the late AI pioneer and learning theorist, Seymour Papert, said when asked what three things he would change about schooling in the age of the personal computer. He replied, "Do away with curriculum. Do away with segregation by age. And do away with the idea that there should be uniformity of all schools and of what people learn."

So far, technology has little to no impact on teaching practices. In fact, one example is how interactive whiteboards are used in classrooms. The vast majority are tethered to a computer in the corner of a classroom that does not allow a teacher to control the board from anywhere in the classroom. The teacher is the one that uses it most frequently and it only replicates a prior teaching practice of writing on a chalkboard. Why haven't air boards become a must-have technical accessory with these interactive whiteboards?

Many so-called education technology practices simply replicate traditional teaching practices. Examples include converting textbooks to digital format and making videos of lectures to post online. Many software programs continue to be "drill and kill" with no adaptations as students progress. Unfortunately, decision makers who purchase technology products for schools are choosing to reduce costs and create efficiencies before transforming teaching practices.

To truly move from teacher-centered learning to student-centered learning requires a major mind shift on the part of teachers. In a teacher-centered classroom, the teacher is the focus, hence the term "sage on the stage." In this one-way communication model, the teacher talks, and the students listen.

Many teachers are comfortable with this model and find it difficult to change their mode of instruction.

Another term that goes hand in hand with "sage on the stage" is the term of "guide on the side." It is meant to represent the transition of using traditional teaching practices to become a facilitator of learning. Unfortunately, teachers think it means giving up their role as content expert and instructional leader. This term misrepresents the teacher's role in a student-centered classroom. The teacher does not relinquish their role but enhances it to enable two-way communication. Moving to a learner-centered classroom includes these examples:

- Focusing on how students use language
- Students interacting with the instructor and with each other
- Students work in pairs, in groups, or alone, depending on the purpose of the activity
- Students talking without constant teacher monitoring
- Students having some choice in topics
- Students evaluating their own learning as well as the teacher.

But a learner-centered classroom is going to be noisier and busier, with students talking and moving around more than usual. Often the physical design of schools and classrooms make this type of instructional practice difficult. However, the most difficult part of moving to this type of classroom is the change of mindset a teacher must make, as well as administrators and others that enter the classroom to coach or observe from teacher to student-centered.

The teachers that have difficulty moving to a student-centered classroom may have misperceptions about what student-centered means. In the extreme misperception, it may mean losing "control" and allowing students to run amok. To other teachers, it may mean learning a completely new set of teaching skills they may not have the will or desire to learn. But as instructional leaders, teachers must move past the fear and be willing to rethink traditional structures and practices such as grading practices and one-size-fits-all curriculum.

PRACTICAL MATTERS

1. *The Maris Mindset List* creates a list every year to examine what defines first-year college students. It was created at Beloit College in 1998 to reflect the world view of incoming freshman and to help faculty understand incoming classes. The most current list is for the class of 2024, or for the freshman

that entered college in Fall 2020. Here are some examples from the Marist Mindset List for that class:

- Incoming students will rely on smart devices for shopping, interactive wellness-centered consumer experiences, and engaging in the social good.
- The class of 2024 may view the idea of "banned books" as an artifact from the past, but the Harry Potter series has been banned somewhere in America for their entire lifetimes, and *To Kill a Mockingbird* has appeared on the American Library Association (ALA) list of frequently challenged books eight times since 2004, due to perceived concerns over offensive language as well as racial and sexual themes.
- Incoming students are willing to pay for their privacy. Privacy is now a commodity, and they value privacy for their real relationships.
- The necessity of personal protection equipment (PPE) will drive fashion trends for the next couple of seasons as young designers in the class of 2024 adapt face masks and other PPE into functional objects of personal expression.
- For incoming students, the world political stage has always been post-9/11; Vladimir Putin has always been the leader of Russia, Tayyip Erdogan has always been leader of Turkey, and the United States military has always been involved in Afghanistan.
- Incoming students are keenly aware of the major threats to the health of our society created by both an international pandemic and the global climate crisis, while at the same time, the value of science in our national dialogue is increasingly questioned.
- Incoming students have never been more ready to embrace social distance by using technology to fill the distance gap. They are always looking for the newest upgrade.

Keep in mind these students have just left high school. These mindsets were formed in their K–12 years by world events and cultural movements: and it is a constantly changing landscape. It is a powerful illustration and reminder of how students who grew up with technology think and process information fundamentally differently from their predecessors.

It is recommended that teachers spend some time with the latest list and have a conversation about how it could apply to their own mindsets. This could lead to a close look into belief systems and other filters we may or not be conscious of when making the transition out of techno centric instruction. Discussion should not be so much about the content in the lists but what that content represents for the way students think about the world. What role do teachers' belief systems play in this context? Are belief systems getting in the way of making effective instructional decisions due to differing mindsets? Difficult conversations for sure but necessary to have with each other.

2. Drs. Judi Harris and Mark Hofer at the College William and Mary have focused years of research on developing a conceptual tool to help teachers match technology integration strategies to how teachers plan for instruction. It is a comprehensive set of learning activity types for each curriculum area with specific technologies that can support the types of learning for each activity. It is an important first step in moving about from techno centric planning. The resources provided on the website activitytypes.wm.edu helps educators operationalize the TPACK framework and makes sure the tail is not wagging the dog: technology coming before the students.

Once teachers plan learning goals, they must make decisions about the type of learning activities that will take place. Learning activity types function as conceptual learning tools for teachers. They describe the learning as it relates to what students will do when engaged in a learning-related activity. Selection of these activity types prior to the selection of technologies is a major mind shift.

Harris and Hofer have developed learning activity types taxonomies in six curriculum areas K–12: elementary literacy, secondary English, mathematics, science, social studies, and world languages. For example, there are 42 social studies learning activities that represent three sets of activity types: knowledge building (such as read text, simulation, or debate), convergent knowledge expression (such as answer questions, create a timeline, take a test), and divergent knowledge expression (such as write an essay, create a mural, or build a model).

In charts on their Wikimedia page, they provide descriptions of the activity types and possible technologies. For example, for the activity type "build a model," the description reads "students develop a written or digital mental model of a course concept/process." Possible technologies include Inspiration, PowerPoint, and InspireData software tools.

It is recommended that teachers find the activity type charts that align with their content area and include them in professional conversations and planning sessions. These charts can be used as a guide at the school level to encourage teachers to make education technology selections based on curriculum-based learning goals rather than the other way around. Perhaps a district-wide chart can be developed using digital tools available to add to the possible technology's category.

Making major changes to the way teachers plan lessons, whether or not technology is used as an instructional tool, will overcome the major obstacle in education reform—changing teachers' processes for making instructional decisions and delivering instruction to their students for optimal learning.

3. Technology holds the key to changing these structures but only if teachers can reimagine their practices. For example, when students use adaptive learning software to practice new skills rather than "drill and kill" software, learning is more personalized for the student. Knowing the difference between these two types of digital tools, as well as being able to question vendors and administrators about this aspect, becomes important to a teacher's role as instructional leader.

4. Technology can also enable mastery-based learning rather than finite grades. This concept is the same as the checking for understanding framework discussed in chapter 4, only taken to the next level. Just as the teacher uses the CFU techniques to know precisely if students are learning during the whole class teaching process, a teacher maintains the data derived from this technique and applies it on a larger scale.

Students continue to be evaluated against curriculum standards, but a student's success is defined by the achievement of expected competencies, not relative measures of performance or student-to-student comparisons. They are given multiple opportunities to improve their work and demonstrate learning progress in multiple ways such as differentiated assessments.

5. Teachers can record online lessons to allow students to view at their own pace. This simple strategy can be a first step in moving from teacher-centered to student-centered.

6. The year 2020 brought teaching virtually into full focus for all educators. It became quickly apparent that there is a difference between materials for in-person instruction and remote learning. AS instructional leaders, teachers can develop lists of each set of materials with information about what is available and what is lacking so it can be provided. A review process can be established so this activity does not devolve into a meaningless activity, but a strong example of how new materials are purchased.

7. It is time for districts and schools to do a full inventory of what programs support learning. What supports are in place to reach out to students not attending virtual classes? Are there tutoring and mentoring services available in several formats that differentiate learning challenges students face in remote learning? Were any family pods for hubs formed during this time that were successful? If so, what were the criteria for participating, what were the outcomes, and how was success defined?

8. Educators should keep in mind that NO digital programs are independent of teachers. The term "blended instruction" should be dissected and discussed in all professional development settings so there is a common understanding of what that looks like in each classroom and where it fits into the overall concept of student-centered practices.

8

Where Do You Go from Here?

If teachers are asked about their professional challenges, they most often will mention lack of funding, lack of parental support, lack of planning time, or lack of respect from the public. All those challenges are real and represent obstacles in improving learning for students. They are added stressors for teachers and contribute to a teacher's overall attitude towards their profession. But they are outside of a teacher's control.

The greatest challenges teachers do control are usually in reference to their students. They want to know their students well, understand differences in their students' learning abilities and capacities, and motivate and encourage students when they underperform. These latter challenges represent the center of the education labyrinth teachers travel in their career and the primary metaphor of this book.

Teachers face continual stress from increased responsibilities and duties. While these additional duties usually are placed on teachers by administrators, policymakers, and parents, oftentimes, these duties come from the demands teachers place on themselves. Teachers are well known for their altruistic personalities and willingness to go the extra mile for their students.

For example, teachers are well known for spending money out of their own pockets to buy supplies for their classrooms. Even when states reimburse a token amount, usually $250 for the school year, teachers will tell you they spend many times that amount. Teachers are also known for spending extraordinary amounts of time planning lessons and grading papers, usually after school, to the detriment of their family life or mental health.

However, while the public has come to expect this behavior from teachers, and may even find it inspirational, teachers do a great disservice to themselves with these actions. This willingness to sacrifice for the students is morally unfair and practically unsustainable. We must ask ourselves as a society why we find this type of sacrifice from teachers acceptable and what we can do to ameliorate it.

Great teaching is not synonymous with sacrifice to the detriment of a teacher's mental health or family life. Great teaching is being able to connect and inspire students in a classroom setting, creating relationships with students around trust. These abilities to connect with students do not develop all at once. Teachers grow these capacities by developing sound pedagogical skills, such as using wait time, and consistently practicing those skills while also demonstrating compassion and understanding towards students.

Vanessa Rodriguez, author of *The Teaching Brain: An Evolutionary Trait at the Heart of Education*, sheds light on the concept of great teaching. Her book is based on the idea that teaching is a developmental process, just like learning is. But teaching is unique because it is dependent on interaction: You can learn on your own, but you need a learner to teach. Rodriguez believes that awareness of all that goes into those interactions is at the center of successful teaching.

Rodriguez includes five distinct "awarenesses" in her framework: Awareness of the self as a teacher, awareness of the teaching process, awareness of the learner, awareness of interaction, and awareness of context. Each is a continuum, and teachers develop them at varying rates. Awareness of self is perhaps the most illuminating. In teacher preparation and professional development, the focus is usually on the teaching process and understanding students as learners, rarely asking teachers to look at themselves in relation to the profession.

Not all teachers should aspire to be "rock star" teachers, but they all should be aware of themselves as teachers and examine their beliefs, their practices, and continually examine the why and how of their instructional decisions. In fact, "rock star" teachers can establish unrealistic expectations that school land district leaders inadvertently perpetuate. Assuming that teachers are going to make unhealthy sacrifices for their students sets a dangerous precedent that must be eliminated.

Focusing on self-awareness will benefit *all* teachers willing to assess their own talents and challenges as teachers and provide reflection on which to improve practice. Establishing a school culture where these behaviors are expected of everyone, not just the "rock star" teachers, is the key to how teachers restore and retain their role as instructional leaders.

PRACTICAL MATTERS

1. Teachers must banish the myth of multitasking. The myth of multitasking, when it comes to paying attention, is not biologically possible. Everyone experiences this inattention when they are listening to a boring lecture, sitting in a tedious meeting, or trying to meditate. The brain starts to wander which greatly erodes attentional ability. Becoming more aware how the brain processes sequentially can inform teachers about how to better manage their time and tasks as well as plan lessons that will keep students' attention.

2. *Remember the 10-minute rule.* Every 10 minutes the brain will disengage unless the communicator takes some action to engage the listener. In faculty meetings, in teaching situations, and other educational settings where information is being relayed, it is important to stop every 10 minutes and provide time for listeners to digest what has been communicated. Educators should be not sacrifice learning for expediency.

3. *Studies show that a person who is interrupted takes 50 percent longer to accomplish a task.* Not only that, he or she makes up to 50 percent more errors. Think about what that means in the classroom when students are called out of class by someone at the door or during loudspeaker announcements in the middle of instruction. Administrators must take leadership in this area to ensure instruction time is not interrupted for any reason and communicate this principle to all staff.

Also think about how that research applies to teachers trying to complete unstructured tasks mentioned previously. Teachers can honor each other's time by not interrupting during these tasks, especially if a teacher has so designated via calendar or physical sign on door.

4. *Teachers can take actionable steps to create a better work-life balance that meet personal and family needs.* Having access to technology 24-7 does not mean teachers should be on call 24-7, allowing technology as a vehicle for administrators or parents to invade personal space. For example, teachers should remove work emails from their smartphones. They can establish "office hours" and set up out of office replies. Administrators should not send after-hour emails except for emergencies—and clearly define "emergency" so all faculty are aware.

5. *Teachers should add visible time in work calendars that clearly delineate unstructured tasks such as writing emails, grading papers, or lesson planning.* It is easy to let time "get away" from you when time for these tasks is unaccounted for. Teachers can establish clear work-home boundaries and honor and respect their own as well as their colleagues.

6. *When new technologies are introduced in a school, teachers should be clear about the type of professional development they need to master.* They should then integrate the tool, if indeed it will add value to instructional practices, not just an efficiency or cost reducing purchase.

7. *Self-care is one of those expressions that makes teachers think of selfishness and self-absorption, the opposite of what they believe the teaching profession is all about.* However, self-care is about teachers taking care of themselves and having what they need to thrive in their profession. Rather than dismiss it as superficial, teachers should regard self-care as something

they deserve. As caregivers, teachers often tell others to take care of themselves rather than do it themselves. Self-care can prevent or reduce teacher stress and possibly prevent burnout. Brainstorm self-care activities that work, then make time for them in your schedule. Find 10–20 minutes in the school day to take a break and decompress. This may seem an impossible task given the frenetic day most teachers have, but this is important. If teachers find that they cannot overcome stress and burnout on their own, it is recommended they seek counseling or another form of professional help. There is no shame in seeking that help. Everyone needs it at some time in their life.

Bibliography

Barshay, Jill. The dark side of education research: Widespread bias. *The Hechinger Report*. March 18, 2019. hecchingerreport.org.

Blackburn, Barbara R. A beginner's guide to understanding rigor. barbarablacburnonline.com

Brown-Martin, Graham. Why don't you design a school? June 20, 2020 Medium.com/regenerative.global.

Carey, Benedict. *How we learn: The surprising truth about when, where, and why it happens.* Random House, 2014.

Cobb, Matthew. Why your brain is not a computer. *The Guardian*. February 27, 2020. theguardian.com

Done, Phillip. *32 third graders and one class bunny*. New York: Touchstone. 2005.

Edpuzzle. Teachers in the movies: The good, bad and the ugly. November 4, 2019. blog.edpuzzle.com.

Ferlazzo, Larry. The whys & hows of activating students' background knowledge. Education Week. June 15, 2020. edweek.org

Festinger, Leon, Henry Riecken, and Stanley Schachter. 1956. *When prophecy fails: A social and psychological study of a modern group that predicted the destruction of the world.* Minneapolis: University of Minnesota Press.

Fishman, Julia. Maris mindset list for class of 2024: New in-depth approach to examining what defines first year college students. Marist. September 9, 2020. marist.edu

Fontaine, Claire. The myth of accountability: How data (mis)use is reinforcing the problems of public education. August 8, 2016 datasociety.net

Fulbrook, Paul. The best types of questions in the classroom. Teachers of Sci. November 14, 2019. teachersofsci.com

Fullen, Michael. *The six secrets of change: What the best leaders do to help their organizations survive and thrive.* Jossey-Bass, 2008.

Fullen, Michael. *Change forces: Probing the depths of educational reform*. The Falmer Press, 1993.

Furey, William. The stubborn myth of learning styles. *Education Next*, 20(3). Educationnext.org

Garmston, Robert J. and Bruce M. Wellman. *The adaptive school: A sourcebook for developing collaborative groups.* 2nd Edition. Christopher-Gordon Publishers, Inc., 2009.

Goodwin, Bryan. Zombie ideas in education. ASCD. May 1, 2021. ascd.org

Gordon, Nora and Carrie Conaway. Asking the right research questions. ASCD. May 1, 2021. ascd.org.

Harris, Judith B. and Mark J. Hoefer. Grounded technology integration: Instructional planning using curriculum-based activity type taxonomies. *Journal of Technology and Teacher Education*: 2010.

Heick, Terry. A visual summary: 32 learning theories every teacher should know. teachthought.com.

Hess, Dr. Karen. Cognitive rigor & DoK focus area. karin-hess.com

Hollingsworth, John and Sylvia Ybarra. *Explicit direct instruction: The power of the well-crafted, well-taught lesson.* Thousand Oaks, CA: Corwin Press, 2009.

Hord, Shirley M. William L. Rutherford, Leslie Huling, and Gene E. Hall. *Taking charge of change.* 2nd edition. Southwest Educational Development Laboratory, 2004.

Koeler, Matt. TPACK explained. TPACK. September 24, 2012. matt-koeler.com

Kolbert, Elizabeth. Why facts don't change our minds. *New Yorker*. February 19, 2017. newyorker.com

Lee, Laura. Teaching isn't a personality contest. Edutopia.org. October 25, 2019.

Marcus, Gary. 2008. *Kluge: The haphazard evolution of the human mind.* New York: Houghton Mifflin Company.

Medina, John. *Brain rules: 12 principles for surviving and thriving at work, home, and school.* Pear Press, 2008.

PowerSchool. SAMR model: A practical guide for k-12 classroom technology integration. April 13, 2021. powerschool.com

Ravitch, Diane. David Berliner: "The required curriculum" vs. "the not required curriculum." The Diane Ravitch Blog. July 29, 2020. dianeravitch.net

Reeves, Douglas B. Leading change in your school. ASCD, 2009.

Rebora, Anthony. The research-savvy educator. ASCD. May 1, 2021. ascd.org

Rodriquez, Vanessa and Michelle Fitzpatrick. *The teaching brain.* New York. The New Press, 2014.

Saaris, Dr. Natalie. Expert strategies to drive greater knowledge in your classroom. Actively Learn. March 19, 2019. activelylearn.com

Sacks, Ariel. What makes a great teacher: Pedagogy or personality? edweek.org. September 25, 2019.

Schmoker, Mike. The obvious path to better professional development. ASCD. May 1, 2021. ascd.org

Shabatura, Jessica. Using Bloom's taxonomy to write effective learning objectives. University of Arkansas. September 13, 2013. tips.uark.edu

Sousa, David A. *How the brain learns.* Corwin Press, 2011.

Varatta, Katie. Teacher-centered v. learner-centered. April 14, 2017. Knowledgeworks.org.

The Wandersman Center. Readiness building systems. wandersmancenter.org

Watson, John. Rock star teachers are a problem for school education systems. digitallearningcollaborative.com. March 4, 2021.

Willingham, Daniel T. *Why don't students like school?* Jossey-Bass, 2009.

Woodford Chris. Technology timeline. Explain That Stuff! March 18, 2021. explainthatstuff.com

About the Author

With a career in education spanning more than 40 years, **Dr. Shirley Ann Smith** has been an elementary and middle school teacher as well as a university undergraduate and graduate instructor. She has led curriculum reform efforts at the state and national levels and created and produced digital resources including online courses, teleconferences, video modules, and virtual field trips used globally. She is a past Fulbright Specialist awardee in technology integration and a past fellow at NASA's Digital Lab. Currently, she is an independent contractor advising schools on how to improve teaching and learning using brain-based research. The greatest joy in her career has been the opportunity to visit teachers in their classrooms and reflect with the teacher on how that data can improve instruction. She has a PhD in elementary education with a minor in education administration from the University of South Carolina–Columbia.

www.ingramcontent.com/pod-product-compliance
Lightning Source LLC
Chambersburg PA
CBHW032029230426
43671CB00005B/253